SCREEN STYLE

SCREEN STYLE

MARNIE FOGG

Front cover Omari Douglas in *It's A Sin* (see p 180)

Back cover top Golda Rosheuvel in *Bridgerton* (see p 114)

Back cover below Jodie Comer in *Killing Eve* (see p 100)

Page 2 January Jones, Elisabeth Moss and Christina Hendricks in *Mad Men* (see p 160)

LAURENCE KING

First published in Great Britain in 2023 by

Laurence King Student & Professional
An imprint of Quercus Editions Ltd
Carmelite House
50 Victoria Embankment
London EC4Y 0DZ
An Hachette UK company

A CIP catalogue record for this book is available from the British Library.

HB ISBN 9781529419719
Ebook ISBN 9781529419726

10 9 8 7 6 5 4 3 2 1

Printed and bound in China by C&C Offset Printing Co., Ltd.

Papers used by Quercus are from well-managed forests and other responsible sources.

Editorial director: Kara Hattersley-Smith
Editor: Carol King
Designer: Geoff Fennell
Picture researcher: Maria Ranauro

CONTENTS

INTRODUCTION

Since the beginning of cinema history in the late nineteenth century, film has been the vehicle by which many fashions have emerged and been disseminated to a wide and eager audience. No longer the prerogative of the big screen, this phenomena has been extended to the small screen, with the role of fashion playing an integral part in the action. The money flooding into TV is the result of a boom in production by US streaming companies such as Disney+, Netflix, Amazon and Apple, TV is no longer the poor relation.

As streaming services compete for relevance and attention, actively positioning themselves as a replacement for the cinema experience, budgets and production values are ever more substantial, including those for costume design, particularly when dramas extend into several series such as *Stranger Things* (see p 48), *Gentleman Jack* (see p 120) and *Euphoria* (see p 54). This allows the designer to work with a bigger budget as the series become successful.

Small-screen dramas also feature eccentric and esoteric subject matter not necessarily appropriate or considered commercially viable on a big screen obsessed

with IMAX-sized special effects. A costume designer is charged with creating a convincing character derived from the abstract text of a screenplay, solely through an illuminating configuration of clothes either created afresh or combined from extant sources. In an immersive visual medium, rooted in the voyeurism of narrative and spectacle, the designer can wordlessly manipulate the latent power of apparel to outline the aspirations, psychology and sentiments of a fictitious or historical character.

Where the actor takes on the mantle of realistic portrayal derived from a script, the designed costume can command subliminal amplification as the willing audience is subconsciously imprinted with the personality traits of the role model – the glamour, the heroism or anti-heroism, even the sheer beauty – which is revealed or reinforced through dress. Female protagonists are made to gain allure by fairytale tropes, like the Cinderella story, as the transformative power of clothes is used to move the character forward, charting their development as they transition through the drama.

Garments are deployed to symbolise various life changes. Visual and dramatic audacity is achieved through

the introduction of the unexpected, as with the murderous seductress Villanelle (Jodie Comer) in *Killing Eve* (see p 100), wearing her frou-frou Molly Goddard layers of tulle.

Designing for different genres requires a different approach, evidenced in the organisation of the book into chapters: Comedy, Coming of Age, Crime, Historical, Retro and Contemporary. Fashion is used to enhance the experience of the viewer: to lighten the atmosphere in a comedy, even for the clothes to be comedic in themselves – as with Moira Rose (Catherine O'Hara) in *Schitt's Creek* (see p 14) – to create tension in a drama, to shift the mood with a change of colour palette or even to signal a change in the direction of a plot. Clothes are deployed to define character: an idiosyncratic role will require whimsical clothes or a strong woman in the political arena will sport sharp-shouldered tailoring, only to don a sexy dress when off duty to emphasise her contradictions or her vulnerability. Sometimes the influence of a look is all pervasive, as with *Peaky Blinders* (see p 80), which continues to exert influence on male dressing. Fashion is never simply used as a mechanism of display, or just as an adjunct to the plot, it is integral to the narrative.

As Polonius says in *Hamlet* (1599–1601): 'For the apparel oft proclaims the man.'

Although Hollywood costume designer Edith Head said that 'motion-picture designers should not deliberately attempt to influence women's style in general', the easy accessibility of what is seen on the small screen provides stylistic inspiration for the viewer. 'What the character wore' websites make it possible to sofa surf and buy into the latest trends seen on a character, transforming the actors into instant influencers. The economic impact of small-screen fashion on the industry is significant. Luxury brands are eager for the association with a fashion phenomenon such as *Sex and the City* (1998–2004) and the follow-on series *And Just Like That...* (see p 32). From being a niche shoe designer, Manolo Blahnik became a household name with the first season; by 2000, the brand was selling 30,000 pairs of shoes at US department store Neiman Marcus alone. Brands have come to understand that TV dramas are far more influential communicators in the arousal of desire than any name that solely appears on the runway or the red carpet; the sofa has become the new front row.

COMEDY

Designing costumes for comedy drama presents an opportunity to intensify the implicit humour of both the cast and the situations in which they find themselves. Clothes may be employed to exaggerate or draw attention to the comedic aspects of a character. They can be used to telegraph or reinforce aspects of a personality that are inherently funny. Comedic effect is achieved through various means: unorthodox silhouettes, changes in proportion – clothes are too large or too small – or a wardrobe that reveals obvious vulgarity or excessive wealth.

Clothes can also designate who is the fall guy, emphasise the blinkered idiosyncrasies of an individual or wittily define the misplaced outsider, such as Moira (Catherine O'Hara), the matriarch of the Rose family in the *Schitt's Creek* (see p 14) series. She is portrayed wearing her out-of-place couture in the local Schitt's Creek diner, adorned with one of her family of fantastic wigs.

This is a dissonant situation familiar to the protagonist in *Emily in Paris* (see p 26), where her every detail is finessed – from the brightly coloured berets to the colour matched accessories; it is an aesthetic in contrast to the chic understatement of her colleagues in the series.

The humour in the comedy drama *Grace and Frankie* (see p 18) is predicated on their divergent personalities, emphasised by the differences in their attire: groomed, high-maintenance Grace Hanson (Jane Fonda) paired with former hippy Frankie Bergstein (Lily Tomlin).

The wise-cracking badinage in *And Just Like That...* (see p 32) accords with the wardrobe decisions of the self-aware protagonists, choices that fuelled an ongoing fascination with the costumes of Carrie Bradshaw (Sarah

above In the comedy drama *Grace and Frankie*, ex-hippy Frankie (right) introduces the polychromatic hand-knitted 'conflict-resolution sweater' from her commune days in an attempt to get her and Grace's ex-husbands, Sol (Sam Waterston, left) and Robert (Martin Sheen), to talk: 'You can't storm off, you have to deal with each other.' It is impossible to overlook the livid rainbow-crafted allusions embedded in this artefact, which is rooted in the Age of Aquarius originating at the height of hippiness at the end of 1960s psychedelic optimism.

Jessica Parker). Humorous incongruity is utilised when the normally graceful and stylish Carrie, ashamed of her smoking habit, dons her special smoking outfit for the benefit of the neighbours when strolling to inhale her single illicit cigarette. Wearing a navy hoodie, Batsheva's enveloping $125 pink gingham house dress, double babushka headscarves and Jimmy Choo's spangled sunglasses with lilac rubber gloves, she is triple-bagged to protect herself, her reputation and her high-end wardrobe from any taint of cigarette smoke. Scenes from the filming of the drama were launched to social media on a daily basis, resulting in luxury brands, including Bulgari, Louis Vuitton, Dior, Prada, Celine and Alexander McQueen, becoming eager to associate with the influential show.

above Distanced by age from the underplayed elegance of her colleagues, and with a physicality resonant of both French author Colette and Sonia Rykiel, doyenne of French fashion design with her wild and curly bob and Left Bank flair, veteran agent Arlette appears as a throwback to the 1970s, the heyday of her youth. She has the advantage of the Chanel-inspired classic indicators of establishment status. She is rendered serious and businesslike by her soft-tailored cardigan jacket, worn coordinated with a closely toned, long dress with a gentle, pearl-trimmed, wide neckline to frame the festooned necklaces – a madeleine pendant and gold chains with a chunky amethyst. She combines these with a whimsical brooch, bold earrings and a bouquet of roses.

CALL MY AGENT!
(DIX POUR CENT)
ANNE SCHOTTE, CARINE SARFATI (2015–2020)

International stars clamoured to play a fictionalised version of themselves in the witty and self-referencing drama *Call My Agent!* The original French title of *Dix Pour Cent* (10%) refers to the cut that agents charge for representation. Created by Fanny Herrero and Dominique Besnehard – drawing from his own experience as the best-known casting agent in France – the series is set in the office of the Agence Samuel Kerr (ASK) in Paris.

For inspiration, French-born costumier, Anne Schotte, researched the wardrobes of agents she knew, whose style she describes as 'professional, yet in the know', adding:

> *'We here are terrified of vulgarity, which leads to little experimentation. The general idea is to build a wardrobe based on time-tested basics: a trench coat, a simple black sweater, a masculine coat, a simple white T-shirt.'*

Carine Sarfati took over costume for the second season from Schotte, who returned in 2018 for the rest of the series. Each episode features a real-life celebrity whose level of fame is concomitant with the increasing popularity of the series as it progresses: Juliette Binoche, Monica Bellucci, Isabelle Huppert and Charlotte Gainsbourg all appear, and are willing to satirise their public image for comedic effect.

The drama opens with the death of the founder of the agency Samuel Kerr (Alain Rimoux) – he swallows a wasp

above Agency staff gather at Agence Samuel Kerr (ASK) with Andréa, central to the group, personifying effortless chic. She is stylish enough to represent actors, yet subtle; her wardrobe is built around timeless pieces such as this narrow fitting, single-breasted, knee-length coat in dark emerald green, a stray toning shade among her wardrobe staples of navy and grey. She is flanked by agency boss Mathias – corporate in his bespoke three-piece suit and tie – the unshaven Gabriel in an open-necked shirt, who represents Bobo culture (*bourgeois bohème*), and Arlette in a classic knitted edge-to-edge jacket in bouclé wool by Chanel. Also in the office are Sofia with her youthful Afro, Noémie the mistress in a vivid orange pin-tucked body-con dress and the unassuming Camille, the office intern, in her jeans and unadorned print top.

left Introduced into the series as Hollywood royalty, Sigourney Weaver avails herself of the starry privileges of entitlement with her challenges and demands. Dressed casually, over a simple white scoop-necked T-shirt she wears a crisp, open shirt in white and indigo, symmetrically pattern-dyed by the *kokechi shibori* technique. This esoteric and expensive dyeing process excludes the indigo pigment from controlled zones by tightly blind-binding areas of the raw fabric before it is placed in the dye bath. At breakfast, Weaver takes objection to her 'senior' suite at her hotel and requires that Camille, self-effacing in her autumnal shades, should cut up her food for her.

below left In a couture, red-carpet evening dress, and in character as herself, Juliette Binoche admits to looking like a 'plucked pigeon', following a series of discombobulating and dishevelling events – a frantic dash to find a lavatory, being shadowed by the security guard from festival sponsor Chopard, fending off the attentions of a Harvey Weinstein-like figure. Despite her serious reservations about the frivolity of the look that has been imposed on her, Binoche nevertheless gathers herself to deliver her keynote address regarding the inclusion of women in the film industry, for which she receives a standing ovation at the glitzy opening of the Cannes Film Festival.

while on holiday in Brazil – and follows the subsequent play for power by the wily senior agent Mathias Barneville (Thibault de Montalembert) and his colleagues Andréa Martel (Camille Cottin), Gabriel Sarda (Grégory Montel) and Arlette Azémar (Liliane Rovère), aided by their assistants Hervé André-Jezak (Nicolas Maury), Noémie Leclerc (Laure Calamy) and Camille Valentini (Fanny Sidney). Agency staff are beleaguered by the caprice of wayward clients, broken contracts, accident-prone film sets and competition from a rival agency, StarMédia. They find themselves cast in supplementary roles – as therapists, babysitters and troubleshooters. At the same time, they are attempting to navigate their personal lives and relationships. Mathias is having an affair with his assistant Noémie, there is a romance between dishevelled idealist Gabriel and aspiring actress Sofia Leprince (Stéfi Celma), and Andréa endeavours to balance the demands of new parenthood with her other new role as agency head.

Andréa epitomises the legendary Parisian archetype – slender, understated, effortlessly sexy yet elegant. Her wardrobe is confined to shades of navy or grey. While her

sharply tailored jackets – often from Zadig & Voltaire or Zara – are fitted at the waist and cropped to show the curve of the hips. Andréa's direct style is a reflection of her managerial responsibilities; she tends to wear her tailored pieces with a plain silk shirt or thin jersey tee, cinched into tight low-rise trousers or skinny jeans, and accessorised with an unadorned, voluminous tote bag. This constraint is offset by unobtrusive make-up, glowing skin, loose shoulder-length hair and perfect legs shod in Christian Louboutin heels. By night, Andréa shows her taste for spine-revealing dresses and, for the Cannes Film Festival opening ceremony, she dons a 1960s-inspired metallic shift dress by Australian designer Martin Grant.

Andréa's insouciant attitude to fashion is not shared by the character Camille, who is the unacknowledged illegitimate daughter of Mathias. On starting her work as an intern at the agency, she is deciding what to wear for her important first day. She despairingly tells her mother, Annick (Isabelle Candelier): 'The girls in Paris are so lissome. I don't know how they do it.' Her mother replies: 'They eat bird seed and scowl, that's all.'

above Relaxing with her feet up in the office, Andréa (left) is informal in a black jumpsuit featuring military detailing in the flapped breast pockets and metallic buttons, which she accessorises with a single silver metal bangle. She allows herself an injection of colour with deep-red suede cowboy boots, a style originally worn by cowboys in Spain and always identified by a rounded pointed toe and a Cuban heel. Gabriel is equally informal in a charcoal grey cashmere sweater worn with jeans and Superga trainers. Arlette is holding her constant companion, Jean Gabin, a canine namesake of the male lead in *La Bête Humaine* (1938).

SCHITT'S CREEK

DEBRA HANSON (2015–2020)

In its final season, *Schitt's Creek* secured a record number of Emmy comedy nominations. Co-created and produced by father and son Eugene and Daniel Levy, it provides a life-enhancing, warm and witty foray into the way an ostentatious and wealthy family cope when they lose all their money and become homeless and poor. Homeless, that is, apart from the rundown town of Schitt's Creek in Ontario, bought as a joke in 1991 by the patriarch of the family, Johnny Rose (Eugene Levy), as a birthday present for his son David (Dan Levy). The series follows the family of Johnny, his soap-opera actor wife, Moira (Catherine O'Hara), and their pampered adult children, David and Alexis (Annie Murphy), as they struggle to adjust. Their town becomes the haven of last resort for the Roses when the Internal Revenue Service (IRS) strips them of their assets after the exposure of the fraudulent machinations of the business manager of their video-store empire. The family are forced to decant from their former mansion into just two rooms in the shabby Schitt's Creek Motel. The vestiges of their former lives reside solely in the wardrobe inventory they have salvaged from the grasp of the IRS and in their enduring sense of entitlement. Costume designer Debra Hanson confirms:

> '*Their money was taken away, their jewellery was taken away, their house, their furniture, what did they have left? All the clothes that they could pack into a trunk.*'

above Actor Catherine O'Hara proposed that Moira's theatricality should take inspiration from the aesthetic of heiress and socialite, Daphne Guinness, British style icon and muse to the late Alexander McQueen. She also favours strictly tailored and monochrome outfits from Parisian couturiers such as Givenchy and Balenciaga. With Johnny, as ever, in sober counterpoint of dark business suit and immaculate white shirt, Moira dazzles in a graphic, houndstooth print in the form of a tailored suit, re-proportioned with both cropped jacket and gaucho trouser by Dsquared2. Each of her many wigs is personalised with a name and they are collectively known by Moira as 'The Girls' – a hirsute menagerie, festooning the wall of her motel room like so many trophies.

opposite The Rose family, Alexis, Johnny, Moira and David in front of their new living accommodation, the Rosebud Motel. David wears his skirt 'that isn't a skirt'. His loyalty to graphic black and white garments chimes with the palette adopted by his mother, Moira, although his degendered fashion experiments of mismatched socks, kilts and shorts are comprehensively eclipsed by Moira's more-is-more styling excesses. She is in couture accessorised with a grosgrain necklace. Alexis provides a contrast in her bohemian-inspired paisley, favouring brands throughout the series such as Isabel Marant, Celine and Chloé. Besuited Johnny, as always, is dressed for business.

left Moira and Alexis share breakfast at their daily haunt, Café Tropical. Alexis consumes a wholesome green smoothie, appropriate to the innocence of her nude-varnished nails and flounced white shirt dress from Self Portrait. In contrast, Moira is more heavy-handed, with black-nailed fingers laden with upscale rings, which add accent to a commanding double button-line, Chanel-style jacket in black. By continuing to wear indulgent designer pieces from their former life of luxury, their adjustment and integration into the rhythms of their rural community at first prove problematic.

centre left David eventually becomes a successful entrepreneur with the opening of the Rose Apothecary selling upmarket unguents with his business partner Patrick Brewer (Noah Reid). His disarming mohair intarsia sweater is one of a flamboyant cavalcade of 180 sweaters over eighty episodes, which were sourced and assigned to David. His extensive wardrobe of graphic textured knits include those designed by Christopher Kane, Marc Jacobs, Alexander McQueen, Givenchy and Yves Saint Laurent.

below left Alexis organises an 'immersive experience' of living crows for the premiere of Moira's film appearance in the psychological thriller *The Crows Have Eyes, Part III the Crowening* taking place in the town hall. Still in their finery, the family go into debrief mode, checking out the public response in their motel room, only to find that the event has gone viral. Star of the show-within-a-show, Moira, is released from her usual excess by a design from Pamella Roland, a floating rose-gold gown, embellished with beading and ostrich feathers. Daughter Alexis shimmers in a sensuous, asymmetrically draped, lamé minidress by Yves Saint Laurent.

opposite In the ultimate episode of the final season, the wedding of David and Patrick is a poignant and joyous occasion, a 'happy ending' for them both. Moira is there to officiate at the nuptials, radiant in a cream, gold-trimmed McQueen gown. Her most fabulous wig, a knee-length, shimmering cascade of white gold, is anchored by a lofty bishop's mitre.

The gleeful hyperbole of characterisation enjoyed by the designer and her assistant Darci Cheyne in defining the externalised identities of the cast of *Schitt's Creek* is a convincing model of the synergies of costume, narrative and character. The designers embraced the proactive contributions made by the principal actors involved – even to the extent that co-creator, co-producer and cast lead, Dan Levy, trawled eBay and Etsy for many of the pieces used in the series. In his role as David, the definitively fluid Sweater Boy in his gothic couture is foil to the persistent orthodoxy of button-down collars and sober business suits from Hugo Boss and Ermenegildo Zegna worn by his father, Johnny.

The series is character driven, the plot lines concerned only with small-town problems and events. The overriding theme is one of due regard to family and friends as they learn to value their time together under duress. As Moira says, 'Mindless bickering is a luxury we may no longer afford.'

Rebranded as the Rosebud Motel, the venue eventually becomes successful enough to be sold on as a franchise across North America. Subsequently – their prosperity restored – the family disperse.

above Remaining true to her hippy past, Frankie's patchwork kimono is worn over a T-shirt, an homage to the late reggae star Bob Marley and a reference to her occasional indulgence in marijuana. Sourced from eclectic outlets such as Harari, Alembika and Bryn Walker, costume designer Allyson Fanger also makes special pieces for Frankie whenever the occasion arises. In keeping with her love of one-of-a-kind craft pieces, Frankie's jewellery is sourced from small-label artisans.

above Grace's formal top-handle handbag, fitted trouser suit and kitten-heeled court shoes are in marked contrast to Frankie's loosely fitting knitted layers, cross-body bag and clogs. These are worn with a hippy favourite, Zouave trousers. Balloon-legged with a low crotch and caught in at the ankle, the trousers are named after the uniform of the French Zouaves, who modelled their uniform on the dress of the Algerian Army. Frankie's wayward greying curls, unlike Grace's perfectly coiffed highlights, also emphasise the women's differing aesthetic and approach to life.

GRACE AND FRANKIE

ALLYSON FANGER (2015–2022)

With an ensemble cast of Hollywood veterans, the comedy drama *Grace and Frankie* created by Marta Kauffman and Howard J. Morris, explores what happens when an unexpected announcement blows apart a four-cornered friendship. Grace Hanson (Jane Fonda) an acerbic and reluctantly retired cosmetics mogul and Frankie Bergstein (Lily Tomlin) a bohemian art teacher in pursuit of all things spiritual are respectively married to Robert (Martin Sheen) and Sol (Sam Waterston), who are partners in a successful divorce practice in San Diego. When Frankie and Grace meet up for dinner with their husbands the men tell their wives that they are gay, that they have been having an affair for twenty years and want to get married. Shocked, disbelieving and angry, the two women take refuge in the beach house that the two couples own jointly, leading to a comedic narrative that sparks the chemistry between Fonda and Tomlin, first seen together in the film *9 to 5* (1980).

The women's opposing personalities are expressed in fashion choices curated by Emmy-nominated costume designer Allyson Fanger. She is dismissive of the fact that the leading ladies are in their eighties:

'At no point do either of them give up their unique style to adhere to "older lady" clothing. For them, that would be giving up their identities to fade into obscurity, to become ordinary, regular,

top left Grace's favoured colourful, crisply tailored shirts are created from vintage printed fabrics and designed and constructed by Fanger. Gently fitted and with bracelet-length sleeves, Grace habitually wears them with a popped collar with the top button undone, to Frankie's exasperation. 'You want to get your head out of your collar,' she remarks. Even Grace's informal clothes define her desire to be perceived as glamorous. Frankie exudes her signature laid-back style in one of her numerous kaftans.

centre left Roland Mouret's expertise at sculpting the body with form-fitting garments was first seen in his iconic Galaxy dress in 2005. His Queensbury cut-out shoulder cape dress exactly fulfils the desire of Brianna (left) to combine sex appeal with sophisticated tailoring when she takes over the helm at her mother's beauty-products empire.

below left Brianna as a new entrepreneur is power dressing in an emerald green trouser suit from the upmarket label Gabriela Hearst. Mallory is in a ba&sh floral-printed, chiffon blouse that emphasises her role as an unthreatening stay-at-home mother. Caught in the middle is Grace, in one of her signature shirts. All three women are blonde but their hair is styled according to their role in the drama: Mallory has soft side-sweeping curls, Brianna has a power bob and Grace has structured highlights layered away from her face for maximum lift.

opposite Exploring alternative futures for Grace and Frankie, the drama imagines that the duo have never become friends. Grace appears wearing a bright turquoise, iridescent silk dupion trouser suit and has had an extreme facelift so that even her ex-husband does not recognise her. She has married a wealthy patio-prince. Frankie has become ever more excessive in her adoption of the bohemian lifestyle with lilac 'locs' (sculpted ropes, similar to dreadlocks) and a sweeping, floor-length kaftan.

predictable, or – at the very worst – completely
thoughtless when it comes to personal expression
through wardrobe choices.'

As befits an alpha female and successful businesswoman, Grace has steely self-control, evidenced by
her high-maintenance routines, and takes pleasure in her
perfection, which is manifested in colour-blocked trouser
suits, crisp shirts and sensuous lingerie by Hanro and
Desmond & Dempsey. Ralph Lauren, Brooks Brothers and
St. John Knits, renowned for their luxurious classic wool
and rayon knits, provide her high-status wardrobe. Her
ex-husband Robert is a similarly conservative dresser,
wearing clothes reminiscent of his preppy days in the
1980s, unlike his more adventurous partner Sol, who
delights in loose, eye-catching shirts. Frankie's freewheel-
ing look is predicated on her days as a hippy in the 1960s.
She chooses comfort over artifice, but has also honed her
personal aesthetic to present herself as an avant-garde
artist, adopting billowing, hand-printed kaftans made from

natural fabrics such as linen, which she adorns with excessive amounts of chunky ethnic jewellery.

Both couples have grown-up children and grandchil-
dren, Frankie's adopted sons are Coyote (Ethan Embry), who
is just out of rehab, and Bud (Baron Vaughn), who takes over
his father's law firm when he retires. Grace's two daughters
Brianna (June Diane Raphael) and Mallory (Brooklyn Deck-
er), initially a stay-at-home mother of four, are usually at
odds with each other owing to their different lifestyles
epitomised by their fashion choices. When Mallory replaces
Brianna as CEO of her mother's company she eschews
Brianna's version of power dressing for high-waisted
tailored Gucci trousers and striped blouses tied with a
pussycat bow or a check tweed jacket with a T-shirt.

FLEABAG

JO THOMPSON, RAY HOLMAN (2016–2019)

above Escaping from the tensions of a celebratory family dinner, Fleabag leaves the restaurant for a moment of respite to smoke a cigarette. Dressing for the occasion, she wears a navy jumpsuit slashed to the waist by London label Love – a brand founded by the designer Teri Sallas and her husband, Lakis, retailed through Topshop.

opposite Fleabag's understated and chiefly monochromatic wardrobe has a Parisian quality, particularly allied to her neat chin-skimming bob. Among the many horizontally striped tops worn throughout, she favours the archetypal Breton top with its origins in the striped shirt once worn by all French navy seamen in northern France. She partners it with a prim and schoolgirlish navy pinafore dress.

The beguiling thirty-something heroine of writer and lead actor Phoebe Waller-Bridge's eponymous *Fleabag* shares her transgressive, self-destructive life by the device of breaking the fourth wall, articulating her insights and asides with an ironic side-eye to the camera. She tries to ameliorate her guilt and sadness at the death of her best friend Boo (Jenny Rainsford) – who stepped into traffic after her boyfriend was unfaithful – by a series of emotionally unfulfilling and masochistic sexual encounters. Her relationship with her sister Claire (Sian Clifford) is equally fraught. Although they are united in grief for their dead mother and ignored by their distant father (Bill Paterson), the siblings live diametrically opposed lives.

Restrained, over-controlling Claire is a successful businesswoman, who wears traditional corporate work clothes and is married to a repellent antiques dealer. As a London urbanite in her early thirties, Fleabag's wardrobe is both practical and affordable. Jo Thompson curated the clothes for the first season, followed by Ray Holman in season two, for which he was nominated for the Costume Designers Guild Awards. He confirms the challenge of taking an already influential series and developing the character's wardrobe to reflect her new emotional status, interrupting her severe colour palette for the occasional vivid print:

top left For the marriage ceremony Fleabags putative stepmother – she is never named – and father confirm their avant-garde credentials. The stepmother in a previous episode remarks on her 'art tour' of Japan significantly influencing her choice of wedding outfit, a jacket based on the traditional form of the kimono. Phoebe's father wears a discreetly eccentric Oliver Spencer suit with a small, pleated ruff customised to fit inside the collar.

below left Claire (left) has a disastrous haircut and she remarks that she 'looks like a pencil'. As a guest at the wedding, the asymmetrical long fringe is pinned back into a hairpiece, with just the short fringe showing. A day of momentous decisions for her, she dresses out of character in a nude lace dress. Knowing that she will be meeting the 'hot priest', Fleabag forgoes her customary navy and black to wear a red, floral print, wrap minidress from Instagram-favourite Reformation.

opposite Fleabag and Boo in their pastel-hued, co-owned guinea-pig-themed café. Both wear the uniform of contemporary young urban women: skinny jeans and T-shirts. Expressing her vulnerability and sensitivity, Boo is the more bohemian of the two, hence the layered tank top, multiple necklaces, tousled hair and big boots.

'You start breaking down the characters within the world that's been created. For Fleabag, it was Fleabag's world. And Fleabag's world was already set up. What I had to do for Fleabag was elevate that world. And take it, move it forward with Fleabag.'

As Fleabag is the hard-up owner of a not very successful café that she initially ran with Boo and then ran alone, she frequently reappears in the same garments throughout the series. Worn consistently throughout both series – even used as a dressing gown at times – Fleabag wears her classic black trench coat from British–Swedish brand Cos. The majority of her clothes are monochromatic and sourced from mid-market high-street retailers such as Benetton, Muji, Cos, Zara and Urban Outfitters, with high-waisted jeans from Arket.

However, for a family dinner to celebrate the engagement of her father to godmother and soon-to-be-stepmother (Olivia Colman) she decides to make more of an effort. Not only has she not seen her family for a year, her sister will be at the event, and Fleabag feels the need for sartorial superiority in Claire's meticulously presented presence and decides on a jumpsuit with a plunging neckline worn with Superga trainers. Also attending the dinner is the handsome and charismatic Catholic priest (Andrew Scott) destined to perform the wedding. Their attraction is instant, fuelled by tins of gin and tonic in the vestry and confirmed when he invites her into the confessional box to confide her greatest fears. Their relationship flourishes then flounders, and after officiating at her father's wedding, the priest ends their affair.

EMILY IN PARIS

MARYLIN FITOUSSI, PATRICIA FIELD (2020–)

D arren Star, the man behind *Beverly Hills, 90210* (1990–2000), *Sex and the City* (1998–2004) and *Melrose Place* (2009–2010), reunites with renowned costume designer and super-stylist New Yorker Patricia Field with her unerring eye for the fantastic for his production of the fashion-led extravaganza *Emily in Paris*. He acted as a 'costume consultant' and, together with the Parisian costume designer Marylin Fitoussi, produced more than 10,000 pieces for the series, a mix of luxury fashion, vintage and emerging labels.

Set against the boulevards and monuments of the City of Light (*La Ville-Lumière*) the comedy series follows Emily Cooper (Lily Collins) as she unexpectedly moves from Chicago to Paris following the acquisition of French luxury marketing company Savoir by US pharmaceutical marketing firm, the Gilbert Group. Her brief is to provide a US point of view and to raise their social-media profile. The wide-eyed *ingénue* is initially scorned and ridiculed by her new colleagues for her woke Midwestern values, her work ethic, her choice of clothes and, above all, for her inability to speak French. She is befriended by: Mindy Chen (Ashley Park), a would-be singer and stylish au pair; Gabriel (Lucas Bravo), a chef who lives downstairs from her; Gabriel's girlfriend Camille (Camille Razat); and assorted French lovers.

Field deploys US stereotypes of France for Emily's introduction to the workplace – ankle boots, a beret and a

above Climbing the five floors to her new apartment, Emily is thrilled with her view of the Parisian rooftops as she flings open the shutters. True to her US roots, she wears an oversize, flannel check shirt. In a drama for the Insta generation, throughout the series she marks all occasions with compelling images, subsequently achieving her desired status of influencer.

opposite With a marked facial resemblance to screen icon Hepburn, Emily's temporary transformation from gauche newcomer to svelte Parisian is complete in this scene as Field creates the 2020 equivalent of Audrey Hepburn's Givenchy LBD (little black dress) in *Funny Face* (1957). A smooth silhouette with a fit and flare off-the-shoulder Christian Siriano gown evidences a new maturity, and is worn with a pair of Agnelle gloves, a rhinestone-studded vintage handbag, some Cosmoparis heels and head jewels by La Compagnie du Costume.

right For her first day at Savoir, Emily chooses a chiffon alice + olivia shirt featuring a print of the Paris skyline worn open over a plain white tee and a snakeskin miniskirt. Patterned pointed ankle boots and the big satin bow tied to the bag add to the overall effect of dishevelment, in contrast to the understated chic of her boss Sylvie, who supplies a sophisticated foil to Emily in her kitsch ensembles.

above On a photoshoot with an about-to-be-naked model on the Alexandre III Bridge, Emily wears a check Veronica Beard short suit, a classic Chanel 2.55 quilt-and-gilt handbag and a red beret. Perceived as representing the archetypal disaffected Left Bank Parisian, the beret was once known as a 'liberty cap' or 'bonnet rouge' (red cap). Its antecedent was the conical Phrygian cap, appropriated by the sans-culottes army of revolutionary France.

baguette – in contrast to the groomed perfection of her acerbic boss Sylvie Grateau (Philippine Leroy-Beaulieu), whose soigné outfits are by Rick Owens, Roland Mouret and Yohji Yamamoto.

It was originally planned that following a shopping trip with Sylvie, Emily would evolve into the perfect French girl but Collins declined to undergo an on-screen transformation. Designer Fitoussi also preferred the character to retain her own idiosyncratic style, asserting:

'Darren Star and Patricia Field have this American idea of French elegance – a body-con dress and high heels. And I think Darren had a little girl in his mind: a nice handbag, nice hair and make-up.'

However, as the series progresses, Field's hand can be seen as Emily's style becomes more redolent of Hubert de Givenchy's muse and screen icon Audrey Hepburn. Chanel is a favoured label throughout the series, including a green

cotton jacket from the Cruise 2020 collection, as well as the pearl-studded quilted bag from spring/summer 2019. Criticised, particularly in France, for promoting stereotypical images of the city and its residents – the rude waiters, the Eiffel Tower selfies – the series nevertheless appeals for its escapist charm, particularly when it moves to other locations such as Saint Tropez in the second season.

above left Emily is a vision in all-over pink, which reflects her relentlessly optimistic nature and is a reference to the Audrey Hepburn film *Funny Face* (1957). In an early scene from the film, the editor of *Quality* magazine Maggie Prescott (Kay Thompson) instructs her staff to 'Think pink! Think pink, when you shop for summer clothes. Think pink! Think pink! If you want that *quel-que chose*.' The double-breasted, drop-shouldered coat has the fit and cut of 1960s couture. Its classic lines are offset with the brief satin miniskirt and black-and-pink-checked mohair jumper. Much maligned pop socks, usually worn under trousers, are matched with stiletto-heeled shoes.

above right In the second season, Emily makes a concentrated effort to learn French, but her wardrobe reverts to her resolutely US love of brilliant colour and matching accessories. A yellow and green Madras check bomber jacket is worn with a traditional Laulhère beret, driving gloves and bag, all in sunshine yellow.

AND JUST LIKE THAT...

MOLLY ROGERS (2021–)

above Putting her apartment on the market, Carrie returns to her old haunts, donning Chanel patent-leather ankle boots and an ankle-length tutu, worn this time around with an age-appropriate striped tee rather than a flesh-toned body stocking seen in the opening credits of the first season of *Sex and the City*. Walking to her local coffee shop, she carries a canvas Ludlow tote bag and the familiar purple-sequinned Fendi baguette bag that a robber memorably snatched from her in the original series.

opposite A showcase of high-end fashion allied to consumerism, the series sees the friends once again striding along the streets of New York – the sidewalk as catwalk – this time minus Samantha. Miranda with her newly bobbed grey hair wears a simple outfit of an unadorned Oleana plaid top by Altuzarra with tapered trousers and Vince pumps by Manolo Blahnik. Throughout the series, Carrie invests in vintage, as in this checked skirt by US designer Norma Kamali worn with shoes by Celine and a hat by Monrowe. Never losing an opportunity to accessorize, her bracelet is by Rosa de la Cruz, and her turquoise and malachite rope necklace by Fry Powers. Charlotte wears an off-the-shoulder dress by Carolina Herrera that emphasises her hourglass figure, patent-leather pumps with floral decoration by Prada and she carries the ABCDior bag by Dior.

From the moment *Sex and the City* first aired in 1998, the lead protagonist Carrie Bradshaw (Sarah Jessica Parker) became a millennial style icon and the original fashion influencer. Based on the book anthology by Candace Bushnell, the groundbreaking female-led drama of four women navigating the dating scene in New York ended in 2004. However, it remains available to watch and continues to appeal, hence the much anticipated reboot *And Just Like That...*, driven by executive producer Michael Patrick King.

Navigating a very different social and sexual climate, the follow-on series picks up on the story of female friendship in the Big Apple as Carrie and her friends – ambitious independent lawyer Miranda Hobbes (Cynthia Nixon) and happy housewife Charlotte York Goldenblatt (Kristin Davis) – hit their mid-fifties. Their personal style remains consistent with their thirty-something selves, with adjustments made through changes in lifestyle rather than age. Discussions regarding ageing are confined to hair colour and the significant facial procedures undergone by some members of the cast are not referenced.

Although Kim Cattrall's much-publicised absence in her role as Samantha Jones from the follow-up leaves a comedic vacuum, this is filled in part by Charlotte's gay friend, Anthony Marentino (Mario Cantone), being given greater screen time. Carrie is now co-hosting a podcast *X, Y and Me*, together with non-binary comedian Che Diaz (Sara

above left The opening scene of the new series sees the three friends shopping for Charlotte's daughters' big night at a piano recital. Direct evidence of product placement is the reference to the US brand Oscar de la Renta seen on the garment bag – Charlotte chooses the label for herself and her daughters. Both Carrie and Miranda wear Dries van Noten, a Belgian fashion designer renowned for his use of colour, print and texture. Carrie's floral bomber jacket is from his 2017 collection, customised for the show, worn over a vintage Claude Montana jumpsuit.

above right Invited to Seema's family's celebration of the Diwali festival, Carrie visits a sari shop in New York's SoHo with Seema, although the items on display are not saris but *lehengas*. Carrie chooses a *lehenga* by Indian couturier Falguni Shane Peacock. Typically, she prefers to expose her toned abs, rather than wear a *dupatta*, a piece of cloth draped over the shoulder to conceal the midriff, originally worn as symbol of modesty.

Ramirez), Miranda decides on a new career path, and Charlotte remains happily married to Harry Goldenblatt (Evan Handler) and they have two children, Lily (Cathy Ang) and Rock (Alexa Swinton), formerly known as 'Rose'.

The drama may be satirising the woke movement – or indulging it – but Miranda, formerly a partner in a law firm who had a relationship with a man of colour, is inexplicably reduced to incoherence in the presence of her African American law professor Dr Nya Wallace (Karen Pittman). This lack of confidence is also reflected in her wardrobe, since she is no longer in corporate suiting but looks deeply uncomfortable in an array of ill-fitting striped and checked garments, the character clearly having difficulty with casual wear.

Costume designer Molly Rogers takes over from Patricia Field for the reboot. She explains her role:

'You can't force someone to wear something. It's a collaborative process. The actor also has to believe in it with confidence, and feel it to be true. Otherwise, they will never pull it off and it will wear them and pull focus from the story.'

Sartorial excitement is sustained with Carrie and two new characters to the drama, Seema Patel (Sarita Choudhury), a realtor she meets when selling the apartment she shared with the deceased Mr Big (Chris Noth), and Lisa Todd Wexley (Nicole Ari Parker), owner of an astounding collection of eclectic and eye-catching jewellery. Wearing a tangerine Valentino gown, from spring/summer 2019, in the final scene of the first season, Carrie takes Big's ashes to Paris using a jewelled bag in the shape of the Eiffel Tower, where she throws them in the River Seine from the Pont des Arts bridge on which Big at last confessed his love for her in the final season of *Sex and the City*.

above left Upping the fashion stakes in the series, in a shocking-pink balloon-sleeved jacket by label Elzinga with matching Louis Vuitton Coussin PM bag and Maxmara acid-yellow shorts, is Charlotte's new friend Lisa Todd Wexley. Dubbed 'LTW', she is a documentarian, humanitarian and fellow parent on their children's event committee. She is also on the *Vogue* international best-dressed list and is an extrovert, keen to dominate each scene with her colourful and exaggerated aesthetic. Eager to impress, Charlotte wears a Zac Posen skirt and carries a Dior Bobby whipstitched bag.

above right Discussing what the future holds following the death of Big, while sitting on the steps of the university where Miranda is studying for a master's in human rights, Carrie admits to finding consolation in walking. 'In those shoes?' Miranda queries. Platform shoes by cult English shoe designer Terry de Havilland are partnered with a 1970s vintage paisley-print maxi dress. One designer handbag is not enough and throughout the series Carrie is double bagged, sporting both Gucci and Balenciaga Hourglass bags.

Get medical attention if Needed and take pictures of injuries...
other identifying info
You don't have to answer any questions from police.
When theyapproach, say "Am I being detained, or am I free to go?" If they detain you, stay silent + demand a lawyer.
A frisk is only a pat down
If police try to do more than that, say loudly, "I do not consent to this search"
iamwetpaint@gmail.com
iamwetpaint.com

HARLEM

DEIRDRA ELIZABETH GOVAN (2021–)

above Angie and Camille are strolling in their neighbourhood when they unexpectedly see Camille's ex-boyfriend.
Dressed in an eclectic array of garments, Angie is
wearing a 1980s-inspired print minidress beneath an
oversized shearling jacket over red leather trousers.
Camille, confident in her fashion choices, channels a
Western vibe in narrow embroidered jeans tucked into
suede drawstring boots, worn with a cropped fur-and-
leather bomber jacket with ribbed cuffs and collar.

opposite Camille is on her way to give a lecture at
Colombia University, ruminating as she walks on the
gentrification of the old Harlem: 'It can be increasingly
hard to hang on to who you are when you can barely
recognise where you are.' Her grey and red plaid trouser
suit, worn beneath a mid-calf classic camel coat from
Pinko and partnered with fringed ankle boots and a
workmanlike tote, exemplifies her professional status.
Her hair is styled in 'locs' – a look closely related to
dreadlocks created by sculpting the hair into ropes.

C reated, written and executive produced by Tracy
Oliver, the sharp, funny drama *Harlem* is one in a
long line of series featuring female friends helping
each other navigate love and life in a big city, such as *Sex
and the City* (1998–2004) and *Girls* (see p 192). Having met at
university ten years earlier, four thirty-something friends –
Camille Parks (Meagan Good), Quinn Joseph (Grace Byers),
Angie Wilson (Shoniqua Shandai) and Tye Reynolds (Jerrie
Johnson) – all live in Harlem, the epicentre of Black culture
and one of New York's most rapidly gentrifying neighbour-
hoods. As professional women, the friends have extensive
high-fashion wardrobes commensurate with their status.

Veteran costume and production designer Deirdra
Elizabeth Govan deploys visual storytelling with metallics,
dyed and printed fur, studded denim, graphic sweaters and
animal prints from labels such as Alexander McQueen,
Marni, Proenza Schouler, Le Superbe and Isabel Marant.
She is also eager to highlight the work of Black designers
including Fe Noel, Brother Vellies, Studio One Eighty Nine
and Wales Bonner, which is evidence of her commitment to
diverse practitioners. Govan recalls the problems she has
encountered in the past:

> 'I could go really on the deep end and talk about the
> struggles being a woman of colour in this business
> and being a costume designer, and it's not easy; but
> at the same time, you have these bright shining

top left Each character in the series has a distinctive style and colour palette. Tye, a successful entrepreneur, is an eager proponent of bright print and the tailored trouser, which is cut with no concessions to femininity. This is combined here in an ASOS Edition jacquard trouser suit constructed from a method of weaving that results in a fabric of complex patterns, which she wears for an important business presentation.

centre left Camille is invited to afternoon tea by her new boss Dr Pruitt, from Yale, but now department head at Columbia University. She is formidable yet fashionable in a dark-brown dress with a floral placement print and a mandarin collar. Her intimidating gaze is intensified by tortoiseshell-framed round spectacles. Eager to impress, Camille wears a demure knitted dress, also brown. Dismissive of her social-media profile, the professor reprimands her: 'If you want to talk about struggle you've got get off your phone and get out into the field.'

below left Camille is invited to the retirement party of the mother of her ex, Ian. She takes Quinn with her for support as he is about to announce his engagement to his girlfriend Mira (Rana Roy). Quinn's notion of party wear is a Sandro formal fitted, bronze metallic, distressed-suede trouser suit, rendered celebratory by the deep *décolletage* of the jacket exposing the bare flesh beneath. Camille projects a more muted approach in a monochrome printed silk dress by Proenza Schouler.

opposite The tribe of 'unbreakable sisters' are all eager consumers of high-end fashion, group affiliation is announced by their sheer enjoyment of clothes, offering a vision of plenitude as they gather together in a nearby bar. Singer and actress Angie is all soft textures, from her Afro hair to a Fashion Nova Fureal jacket in an eye-catching lime. Trust-funded aspiring fashion designer Quinn wears a floral-print, pleated dress from Derek Lam. Camille is the sexy, cool professor in shimmering sequins. Entrepreneur Tye favours a form-fitting, knitted ribbed dress.

lights – or "angels" as I call them – producers and directors who see your value and see your work... [For] me it's definitely been about being in the right place at the right time, but it's also about having the skill set to back it up.'

Camille, whose voice bookends every episode, is an assistant anthropology professor at Colombia University. Her fashion choices have an element of striking theatricality suitable for appearing on the podium of the lecture hall. She is ambitious for a tenured position, and is perturbed when her previously supportive boss is replaced by Dr Elise Pruitt (Whoopi Goldberg) who is unimpressed with her attitude when she turns up late for a meeting showing inappropriate cleavage – her lurex-striped minidress is by Balmain – after sleeping in. With a basilisk stare, Dr Pruitt refuses to endorse her application for tenure. Devastated that her life plan is no longer viable, Camille is also hoping to reconnect with ex-boyfriend Ian Walker (Tyler Lepley), who unexpectedly returns to Harlem after several years abroad to work as head chef in a French-fusion bistro, a move that Camille considers is contributing to the gentrification of the area.

Professionally successful, digital mogul Tye, advocate of the tailored trouser suit, is the lesbian founder of the first dating app for queer people of colour but is in a relationship with a white woman. Angie, a bohemian free spirit with an adventurous personal style, is attempting to re-launch her singing career after being dropped from a record deal four years previously and is financially supported by struggling fashion designer Quinn, whose default setting is sweetly pretty dresses by high-end labels such as Alexis Rozalya and Australian label Zimmermann. Quinn, in turn, is bankrolled by her wealthy mother Patricia (Jasmine Guy).

Various dating disasters ensue in the women's search for love. In the unresolved ending to the first season, Camille is torn between her love for her ex and Jameson Royce (Sullivan Jones), the perfect man of her dreams, who wants her to move with him to Chicago.

ONLY MURDERS IN THE BUILDING

DANA COVARRUBIAS (HULU 2021–)

Created by Steve Martin and John Hoffman, *Only Murders in the Building* is a satire featuring the familiar trope of the amateur sleuth working within a limited cast within a confined space. A fire alarm in the prestigious Arconia apartment building on New York's Upper West Side prompts neighbours Charles-Haden Savage (Steve Martin), an ageing star of TV cop show *Brazzos* with a bleak personal history, Martin Short (Oliver Putnam), an impecunious, unsuccessful Broadway director, and Mabel Mora (Selena Gomez), a disconsolate loner, to meet for the first time. They bond in a café over a true-crime podcast while fellow resident Tim Kono (Julian Cihi) dies in mysterious circumstances. When the police sign off the death of the neighbour as suicide, the trio decide to pursue their own enquiries and record their findings for a podcast in the hope of becoming viral superstars. A convoluted plot line follows as all the inmates of the building take their turns in being accused of Tim's murder.

Costume designer Dana Covarrubias elucidates the process of designing for the drama:

> 'With Selena, my main colour inspiration for Mabel was the marigold, so reds, golds and yellows. We were trying to figure out a way to represent her Mexican heritage – just like Selena, I'm also from Texas and I'm half Mexican... The marigold is really significant iconography of Mexican culture.'

Mabel is a young assertive woman, fond of space-dyed knits, plaid kilts, cropped knits, a glossy leather trench coat and a red utility jumpsuit from MKT Studio, all partnered with a variety of heavy-soled ankle boots including those from Stella McCartney. Charles' wardrobe is predominantly in shades of cool blue, including his distinctive pork-pie hat, in a reference to his initially unapproachable demeanour. The flamboyant Oliver retains his high-end wardrobe from past theatrical successes.

above 'Really, do you not see this coat?' says Oliver as he jaywalks along the Manhattan streets, daydreaming about his Broadway past. His theatrical, intensely textured, colourful and patterned clothes include a purple wool coat by Colombian-born French designer Haider Ackermann worn with a coordinating silk scarf and navy turtleneck. His outfit is a reminder of his more successful days when he could afford to wear clothes by high-end designers such as Prada and Givenchy.

above The colours of autumn in New York are the backdrop to Mabel's choice of red, orange and yellow for her cropped, faux-fur jacket by US designer Michael Kors, in marigold. This is matched to a yellow sweater and plaid trousers, both sourced from Brooklyn vintage stores. She regularly wears the same outfits throughout the series, in keeping with her financial circumstances.

left Charles wears his customary air of bafflement alongside his stunt double Sazz Patiki (Jane Lynch) from his successful TV detective series; she is in town for the stunt-double awards ceremony. Although they share physical measurements and identical outfits, the hang of their clothes exemplifies their differing attitudes to life.

COMING OF AGE

T he peak of the post-war baby boom in 1947 resulted in an unparalleled number of teenagers reaching puberty in the 1960s. In the midst of unprecedented affluence, this generation would come to face a rapid change in culture, with upheaval in social stratification and in institutional, personal and familial relationships. Evolving media industries responded to the stimulus by setting out to harvest its profit potential thanks to a bumper crop of new consumers. Broadcast media took note and hit on the idea of producing material aimed directly at young people. However, it took until the 1990s for multichannelled, deregulated TV companies to develop genres that recognised the income at the disposal of those indulging in an increasingly stretched youth.

The enormous international success of *Beverly Hills 90210*, produced by Aaron Spelling in 1990, proved to be the tipping point in the rise of teen dramas. It had high production values, a cast of wealthy teens and was a vehicle for marketing fashion brands and for promoting music. The template for the coming-of-age genre was established and taken up by a plethora of similarly conceived productions: *My So-Called Life* (1994–1995), the TV series of *Clueless* (1996–1999), followed by the most successful of them all, *Friends*, which was set in New York, first appearing in 1994 and gaining global popularity, airing continually until 2004.

Teen and young adult dramas such as *Stranger Things* (see p 48), *Euphoria* (see p 54), *The O.C.* (see p 58) and *Sex Education* (see p 74) continue to focus on interactions within a group of friends. Inevitably, character profiles are silently defined by the clothes worn and by their implicit cultural relevance. Prevailing stereotypes are legion – the nerd, the bitch, the rebel, the jock, the eccentric, the sexually ambivalent – and all explore and expose their character with the aid of the costume designer. Across the spectrum of series and casts of characters, even including those who

above Based on the novel series of the same name written by Cecily von Ziegesar, the archetypal teen drama, *Gossip Girl*, features a cast of privileged characters living on New York's Upper East Side. The series provides a glossy template for the aspiring fashion-obsessed teenager. Serena van der Woodsen (Blake Lively, left) is attired in a mild version of steam punk and goth; a studded construction anchors the skirt and a fluid drapery of chiffon is caught up at the waist. Blair Waldorf (Leighton Meester, right) is similarly event-attired in a black voile dress studded into place by a grid of *diamanté* spots.

were stereotyped, there is robust traffic in models for feeding the desire for instant gratification for garments purchased impulsively – even mid-episode – from specialist websites or directly through social media.

Significantly, *Gossip Girl* (see p 62) costume designer, Eric Daman, deliberately set out to dress the series as if it was a fashion magazine. Over the six seasons (2007–2012) of the original series, social media exploded with the arrival of the iPhone in 2007, giving even greater impact to the fashions proposed by Daman. It took until the dazzling success of the first season had become self-evident for the global fashion industry – including Parisian couture – to recognise that a commercial genie had been unleashed and thereafter to volunteer merchandise for subsequent and other series.

above Within the perimeter of a few drab suburban streets in working-class Naples, young Elena (left, Elisa del Genio) and Lila (Ludovica Nasti) are free to roam. However, after braving the dark tunnel that leads to freedom and the sea, Lila unexpectedly turns back; she needs the reassurance and familiarity of their own neighbourhood. With identical tousled bobs, homemade shabby dresses and cardigans felted with washing and wear, their only alternative clothing is the severe uniform of their school, a black dress with a white Peter Pan collar and matching buttons running up the back.

opposite This shot, taken on set, shows the girls wearing their best clothes as they visit the city centre. Nonetheless they do not feel sufficiently smart to venture into the Via Chiaia, a retail arcade full of expensive products. Lila (left) insists she wants to buy an ice cream; her friends demur but are persuaded to enter the arcade. Constraint on social mobility is one of the themes of the drama, epitomised when a jealous Rino – in his casual open-neck shirt – insults a well-dressed Neapolitan in white tennis sweater and boater. The man declares that Rino is a ruffian and a fight ensues with Marcello coming to the rescue.

MY BRILLIANT FRIEND
(L'AMICA GENIALE)
ANTONELLA CANNAROZZI, SONIA TRAVAGLIA (2018–)

Based on the acclaimed Neapolitan novels of Elena Ferrante and adapted for the screen by Saverio Costanzo, *My Brilliant Friend* (*L'amica geniale*) begins in the streets of a bleak and colourless post-war Naples and ends in the 1970s, recalled in part from the perspective of 2010. The drama is a *Bildungsroman* – a genre that frequently links personal growth to broader social issues. It examines the dynamics of friendship between two girls, Lenuccia 'Elena' Greco (Margherita Mazzucco) and Raffaella 'Lila' Cerullo (Gaia Girace), known to each other as 'Lenù' and 'Lina', from their first meeting at the age of six, through to adulthood, charting their continual struggle to lead independent lives at a time when women and girls were expected to defer to their fathers, brothers, husbands and priests.

Both girls are academically ambitious and they are determined to leave their bleak impoverished neighbourhood. Their childhood has an undercurrent of menace, the Camorra (Neapolitan mafia) is ever-present and the girls witness violence in the murder of Don Achille Carracci (Antonio Pennarella), a dealer in the black market. With family support, Elena is able to further her education and enrols in high school in Naples. However, Lila, in spite of her superior intellect, has to leave school and work for her shoemaker father, together with her brother Rino (Gennaro De Stefano).

Costume designer for the first three series, Antonella Cannarozzi, is at pains to create an authentic depiction of the period.

'The photos of the time, the first women's magazines, the films shot in that period, the books, obviously the newspapers: everything was very useful to reconstruct the Italy of those years, its transformations... After this phase of research and study we moved on to the practical part... to dress the protagonists, the main characters and a myriad of extras. The vintage that you can find in the shops is not very much... many things have been tailor-made especially for the protagonists.'

Elena is dressed in loosely fitting clothes – dull, pleated skirts and cap-sleeved blouses – in drab colours, all garments enabling her disappearance into the background. She has an unflattering hairstyle and fingers her acne constantly. By contrast, Lila projects a sensuous image, confident in her sexual allure, wearing fitted tops and swirling skirts. She inspires great passions and is beset by the attentions of two men both of whom wish to marry her. Marcello Solara (Elvis Esposito) is a handsome bully who patrols the neighbourhood in his Fiat 1100, acting as an enforcer for his father Silvio (Antonio Milo); his rival is Stefano Carracci (Giovanni Amura), the son of the murdered black marketeer, Don Achille. Meanwhile, Elena goes to work on Ischia. Tanned, and with her hair pulled up in a high ponytail she experiences a brief blossoming, particularly with the attention offered by a school friend whom she had admired from afar, Nino Sarratore (Francesco Serpico). She leaves the island abruptly when his father sexually assaults her and she goes home to help Lila resist the attentions of Marcello. As a way of insinuating himself into the Carracci family, he professes interest in a pair of shoes that Lila has designed. However, with the urging of her father, she favours Stefano, once he promises to invest in the shoemaker's shop. For sixteen-year-old Lila, marriage seems to be the only route out of poverty. The shoes come to play a pivotal role in the story: from being the product of her father, the local shoemaker, they go on to being manufactured in volume and sold in a prestigious location in Naples. The shoes were made for the series with the collaboration of Pierpaolo Piccioli, the creative director of Valentino. The lives of the girls diverge, Lila leaves Stefano to live with Nino, only for him to abandon her and their unborn child and Elena graduates from the University of Pisa and becomes a writer.

top right Lila learns at her wedding reception that her new husband has reneged on a promise to have nothing to do with the criminal Solara brothers. At the hotel in Amalfi chosen for their honeymoon she wears her going-away dress – a lilac sleeveless shift – but her desire to give the appearance of sophistication is foiled by the ineptitude displayed by her new husband, Stefano, in dealing with the staff of the smart hotel. She is embarrassed and repulsed as he greedily devours the meal. On their wedding night she refuses to play the obedient wife, and he responds by raping and assaulting her.

centre right A graceless Stefano dons an Italian-collared, open-neck sports shirt, which is a well-worn screen signifier of delinquency and low-life mayhem as attested by thick-necked heavies in many a crime saga. He wears it with a classic natural linen suit, a look in post-war Italy that insinuates overtones of the *demi-monde*, gained from the raffish glamour of Cinecittà luminaries such as Vittorio De Sica. Following a template of gamine elegance set by Audrey Hepburn in her little black dress, big black shades, headscarf and updo, Lila sits disapprovingly besides him.

below right Elena gives broad credit to her boyfriend, Franco Mari (Bruno Orlando), for being her mentor: 'He has taught me how to love, to study, to have fun.' Dashing through the streets of Pisa to avoid their classmates, they find refuge in the mahogany tones and refinement of a nearby fashion emporium. With his own bourgeois tastes rooted in a gentle reprise on British tailoring and Ivy League nuances, he has helped her define her new, considered, fashionable look. Unfussily accessorised by horn-rimmed glasses and tan leather shoulder bag, her smoothly cropped hair combines with her stylish, understated clothes.

opposite At the celebration of her engagement to Stefano – a solemn rite of passage requiring wine and an abundance of *sfogliatelle* pastries, cream puffs and cannoli – Lila shows off her ring to their families. Unhappy with her decision to marry for financial security, she nevertheless attempts to present a glamorous front with an all-concealing navy blue silk dress and a smoothly domed updo. Lila's mother Nunzia (right, Valentina Acca) and Elena's mother Immacolata (Annarita Vitolo) are clothed in woollen dresses in sombre colours.

STRANGER THINGS

KIMBERLY ADAMS-GALLIGAN, MALGOSIA TURZANSKA,
KIM WILCOX, AMY PARRIS (2016–)

above Eleven has telepathic and psychokinetic abilities. She flees from her incarceration at the Hawkins National Laboratory where she been a test subject of Dr Brenner, where her hair was buzz cut to create a uniformity alongside the other subjects. On her escape, she undergoes a makeover by the friends, who plunder the dressing-up box and replace her hospital gown with a pink smocked dress with a Peter Pan collar and a navy blouson.

opposite above The boys disperse on their BMX bikes following an evening playing Dungeons & Dragons in the basement of Mike's home. His friend Dustin habitually wears a trucker cap and a graphic T-shirt. Lucas has a more developed sense of style, wearing a colour-matched top and trousers beneath his brown hooded coat. Will wears multilayered T-shirts beneath a flannel plaid shirt and sleeveless padded gilet.

opposite below Sharing a cigarette and reminiscing about their shared school days, Will's mother Joyce (Winona Ryder) and chief of Hawkins Police Department, Jim Hopper (David Harbour), sit at her kitchen table in a room suffused with an eerie, sepia light. The claustrophobic low ceiling, shrouded windows and homely 1970s décor of plastic, floral patterned chairs and brown laminate furniture add to the threatening atmosphere. The authority of his well-maintained uniform is set aside by the off-loaded hat and jacket, while Joyce's attire is made yet more casual by the rolled-back cuffs of her shirt.

The mundane tedium of life and culture in the expanses of the American Midwest have long provided a milieu for the other-worldly and laid open the imagination to games of make-believe. Cold War conspiracy theories proliferated in the 1980s – from alien interventions to strange scientific experiments to covert operations. They are all called upon to furnish the back story for *Stranger Things,* the supernatural horror saga by the Duffer brothers, Matt and Ross, set in the fictional rural town of Hawkins, Indiana. The series also gives more than a nod to the films of that era, such as Steven Spielberg's *Close Encounters of the Third Kind* (1977) and *E.T. the Extra-Terrestrial* (1982). In *Stranger Things*, three boyhood friends, group leader Mike Wheeler (Finn Wolfhard), Dustin Henderson (Gaten Matarazzo) and Lucas Sinclair (Caleb McLaughlin), are intent on finding their missing friend, Will Byers (Noah Schnapp). They join forces with teenagers Jonathan Byers (Charlie Heaton) and Nancy Wheeler (Natalia Dyer), helped by Eleven, aka Jane Hopper (Millie Bobby Brown), a taciturn shaven-headed enigma, fugitive from a mysterious scientific establishment that is headed by the sinister Dr Martin Brenner, aka Patient 001 (Matthew Modine).

The costume designers for the first season, Kimberly Adams-Galligan and Malgosia Turzanska, scrutinised films, catalogues and magazines such as *Seventeen* and *Cosmopolitan*, as well as family photo albums and school yearbooks

previous When blindfolded, Eleven has the power to see other dimensions. Mike, Will, Max and Lucas urge her to find her missing adopted father Hopper as they need his help to slay the malevolent entity the Mind Flayer. Mike wears a solid colour top to differentiate from Will's younger look of horizontally striped polo. Californian-born Max favours sporty hoodies and track pants, based on popular 1980s beach-inspired labels such as Ocean Pacific.

above Starcourt Mall, home of the Scoops Ahoy franchise, provides the backdrop and ice creams to the mall-rat teenagers, recently joined by Californian Max. Here, Max is wearing a sunny, sports-striped tee. She has been providing fashion advice to Eleven – usually to be seen in one of her adopted father's oversized plaid shirts. To the tune of Madonna's 'Material Girl', Max and Eleven experiment with assorted print tops and dresses and multiple accessories for a photo shoot. Eleven eventually chooses a boldly patterned, Matisse-inspired, belted minidress.

for inspiration and period authenticity. Featured are big hair and frazzled perms, vibrant prints influenced by the works of Henri Matisse or of New York graffiti artist Keith Haring, and Madonna-inspired lace gloves and marabou feathers. The continuing chronicle celebrates the rise of mall shopping and mall culture in the 1980s, with the allure of an array of retail outlets such as Gap and JCPenney collected in one place. As the Midwest is not notably fashion-forward and Hawkins neither metropolitan nor affluent, residual 1970s influences remain. The group also wear heritage labels from the 1980s such as Wrangler, Lee and Levi's, paper-bag waisted trousers in a light denim wash and cut-off denim shorts. Double denim, tropical prints and drawstring trousers add to the mix.

The drama recounts how, in a nocturnal grid search of Hawkins, the boys scour the terrain on their BMX bikes, in adherence to the familiar Spielberg trope of middle schoolers acting independently of parental authority. Eleven, who happens to have psychokinetic abilities, accidentally opens a portal to a parallel dimension, the Upside Down, and lets loose the Mind Flayer. This abominable incarnation from the

boys' habitual role-play game, Dungeons & Dragons, wields supreme control and spreads the Upside Down's toxic biological growth in the depths of subterranean Hawkins. It has also abducted Byers and rules an army of Demodogs in an undiluted challenge to suspended disbelief. The transcendent occurrence leads to subsequent paranormal activities and a dramatic resolution as the Mind Flayer is duly defeated in a seismic explosion at the mall.

As the storyline develops over the course of the decade, both the interiors and the fashions become lighter and brighter. The second season, set in 1984, has Kim Wilcox as designer, who enjoyed an augmented budget. This appointment was followed for the third series, set in 1985, by that of Amy Parris, brought in to oversee the costumes for increasingly fashion-led episodes.

above Graduated from high school, Steve Harrington (Joe Keery, centre) is working at the mall in the kitsch ice-cream parlour, Scoops Ahoy. His previous Flock of Seagulls hairstyle – invented by a Liverpool hairdresser-turned-band-member in 1979 – has morphed into a bouffant held in place by Fabergé Organics and four puffs of Farrah Fawcett hairspray. For workwear uniform – a pastiche of nautical attire, he is compelled grudgingly to wear stripe-hemmed shorts with a sailor blouse, called a 'middy' – a term derived from naval midshipman. The uniform ensemble worn by Robin Buckley (Maya Hawke, left) has a puff-shoulder matelot top, worn with pleat-front shorts with gold buttons up the sides. Dustin, by contrast, is a free entity, wearing one of his collection of graphic tees, and his favourite yellow, orange and green trucker hat.

above Rue's preoccupations are internalised, focused elsewhere, but she remains fashion-aware, in spite of her downward spiral into addiction. Her dark-toned look consists mainly of comfortable dense layers, as in this Op-art print top, a genre of pattern first made popular in the 1960s with the emergence of artists such as Bridget Riley and Victor Vasarely. Converse high tops, worn with contrarily logoed Vans socks, emphasise her relaxed teen overtones. Jules is fluffily and flimsily clad in her typical delicate shades.

above Lexi, Rue's childhood friend, constantly compares herself to her beautiful and seductive older sister, Cassie. In consequence, she deliberately dresses in a more restrained way. Her dress is an eloquent indicator of her desire for a pretty, constrained femininity. Trimmed with broderie Anglaise, the white pique collar and cuffs frame a red, white and blue plaid bodice, attached at the waist to a bias-cut skirt, redolent of a child's prim party frock from the 1950s.

EUPHORIA

HEIDI BIVENS (2019–)

Created and written by Sam Levinson, *Euphoria* is loosely based on an Israeli TV series of the same name. The angst-ridden drama is fuelled by explicit scenes of sex, both coercive and consensual, of nudity, violence, paedophilia, domestic abuse, alcoholism and drug addiction – all topics introduced in a such a way that dysfunctional and violent behaviour is normalised. With an all-pervasive 1990s fashion influence in the flirty fabrics, body-con dresses, A-line miniskirts and midriff-baring tops, the personalities of all the characters are mediated through their fashion choices determined by costume designer Heidi Bivens:

'In these jobs, you're expected to mood board, because you have to show the director and your team the visual direction you're taking. But honestly, the way that I get ideas is so random. It's not like I'm coming to social media and finding stuff. I'll be walking down the street and see someone who has amazing style, or an image that catches me by surprise. I'll save images to my phone, and over time that evolves into the inspo.'

The drama revolves around a group of high-school-age friends, with lead character Rue Bennett (Zendaya) as the middle-class narrator, a self-destructive seventeen year old. Following a period in rehab after an accidental overdose she befriends Jules Vaughn (Hunter Schafer),

top left When Kat discovers that a video of her sexual activities at a party is circulating online, she decides to exploit her notoriety and becomes a camgirl, catering to the appetites of a series of submissive men with domination fantasies. She confidently contextualises her everyday fashion choices with the impedimenta of her S&M practices, such as a leather harness and choker. Her severe, dark bob contrasts interestingly with the sunny graphic parrots embroidered on her tight, transparent, Jean Paul Gaultier top.

centre left The clothes Jules chooses to wear are not merely a fashion statement but a reflection of her emotional disarray. She is at once a little girl, without responsibility for the paedophiliac response courted by her appearance. Resonant of her fragile personality, her preferred aesthetic is one of *ingénue* frills and colours, with intimations of babydoll whimsicality. Complicated transparent layers are made up of a spangled mesh top, banded in sugary pinks, in turn worn beneath a satin slip with a ruched, embroidered tulle bib. Rue is in her low-key, loose, cotton moleskin jacket.

below left The group attends a New Year's Eve house party, where Rue has a drug relapse and nearly dies, and she and Jules confess their feelings for each other. For this occasion, Maddy wears a black dress with cutouts by Mexican-born designer Aidan Euan (AKNA). It is a throwback to the 1990s body-con silhouette, providing minimal coverage with maximum exposure.

opposite By aspiring to emulate screen sirens such as Brigitte Bardot – famed for her beauty and sexually emancipated lifestyle – Cassie is expressing her need to be found desirable. A soft pink, cropped cable sweater with a plunging *décolletée* and frilled hem makes evident the significance of her bed-head hair she wears to the party. The kittenish vision is completed with snug, midriff-baring, ice-blue jeans.

a transgender girl and newcomer to the town of East High-land, who is attracted to older and overtly homophobic men. This includes Cal Jacobs (Eric Dane), father of Nate (Jacob Elordi), the high-school jock whose default position is one of anger and who is abusive to his girlfriend Maddy Perez (Alexa Demie).

The predilection of Jules for transparent fragile layers is an exposure of her feelings of vulnerability. Rue, usually in a favourite hoodie by fashion brand Alix NYC, tie-dye T-shirts or her dead father's burgundy leather jacket, seeks comfort and familiarity.

A slew of characters constitute the core group: Rue's drug dealer Fezco (Angus Cloud); fan-fiction writer and camgirl Kat Hernandez (Barbie Ferreira), who has issues with her weight; Rue's childhood friend, Lexi Howard (Maude Apatow), and her older sister Cassie (Sydney Sweeney), together with Cassie's ex, a young football player Chris McKay (Algee Smith). A pivotal episode in the second season unfolds as the group attends a New Year's Eve house party. For this occasion, Rue wears a combination of vintage and thrift-store pieces; a Jean Paul Gaultier vest over a thermal top with trousers by Roberto Cavalli. Claudia Schiffer simulacrum Cassie adopts baby blue and pink in House of CB (Celeb Boutique), a British womenswear brand, worn with white Prada heels from The Real Real. The activities of the group are all recorded by dexterous camera angles alongside a high-powered soundtrack that moves the action on in fragmented haste.

above Body-confident Summer Roberts (Rachel Bilson, left) exhibits her midriff between the higher reaches of her skintight, low-rise jeans drawn taut by a channelled denim coulisse and the gathered hem of a cropped, white lace 'Bardot' blouse. Seth (left) and Ryan are identified by their divergent styles. Seth is in a loose print shirt buttoned up to the neck. Ryan – who is a shoe-in for James Dean or Bruce Willis – wears an open shirt over his customary singlet, with a wide buckled belt on his jeans above heavy black boots, both of which are handy in a fight or on a shift in a wood yard. Marissa is sweetly feminine, a less overtly sensual foil to Summer in a lingerie-inspired camisole top and low-rise cargo trousers in distressed cotton moleskin.

THE O.C.

ALEXANDRA WELKER, KARLA STEVENS FLANIGAN,
ROBIN LEWIS WEST (2003–2007)

The sun and surf of Orange County, California and the boat-filled harbour of Newport Beach provides the setting for *The O.C.*, one of the most watched and influential teen dramas; it ascended to the pop-culture stratosphere with season one in 2003. Created by Josh Schwartz, the drama involves a search for family and identity which sees Ryan Atwood (Ben McKenzie), the disaffected and anguished lead-in character abandoned by his mother, with his father and older brother both in jail. He is adopted by the wealthy and philanthropic Sandy Cohen (Peter Gallagher), a left-leaning public defender, and his wife Kirsten (Kelly Rowan). He bonds with their son Seth (Adam Brody), an equal social maladroit and the butt of a group of water polo-playing jocks. The two boys develop a pivotal relationship throughout the drama. The series investigates how they navigate their way through the upper echelons of a materialistic and hedonistic culture, characterised by drink- and drug-fuelled parties, easy violence and the disparagement of the eccentric or different.

In season one, costume designer, lecturer, writer and stylist Alexandra Welker captured a uniquely Californian mix of accessible and high-end clothing with each character defined within these parameters. Welker has a firm handle on the core mechanics of her trade:

'Costume design is just visual shorthand for who we
are and where we're from and what we're going

above Seth confirms his nerd credentials in casual needlecord jeans and a sweater donned to celebrate Chrismukkah, a Cohen family tradition, the result of his father being Jewish and his mother Christian. Though neither religion scores highly on orthodoxy in ecumenical ambition, the tiny menorah-esque border motifs must trump the non-specific universality of the reindeer, trees and snowflake story. The holiday jumper gained popularity in the 1980s and has subsequently achieved popular high-camp status. For her part, Summer's soft pleated top suggests a wintry cascade of polka dots evoking snowflakes.

top left Dressed formally for the cotillion – a garlanded rite of passage initially derived from formal aristocratic balls in eighteenth-century France and England – Summer loosely interprets the prescribed debutante uniform as her full-length white sheath dress in Duchesse satin and opera gloves. At the mock wedding, the debutantes are escorted by their father and handed over to their 'white knights' or male partners.

below left Pining for Summer, his unattainable crush, Seth wears a fitted shirt in forest-green cotton sateen. To suggest the anxieties caused by his unrequited love, the costume designer, referencing the 1970s, gives Seth a tenser, constricted silhouette in contrast to the easy-fitting clothes of his high-school contemporaries, the water-polo playing jocks. Summer does little to suppress her allure as she wears a claret bustier top in ruched, metallic jersey with spaghetti straps and a novelty feature chain necklace, a typical accessory favoured by the female cast of characters.

through in our lives. It's our hopes and dreams and aspirations and all that other stuff we don't necessarily realise we're telegraphing.'

Ryan first sees love interest, Marissa Cooper (Mischa Barton), while standing in the driveway of the Cohen's mansion. Wearing a white V-neck T-shirt, grey hoodie, black leather jacket and a single strand of rawhide leather tied around his neck, he epitomises potential bad-boy broodiness. Despite the influence of his new upper-class family – and the offer of Gucci, Armani and Versace buys on a shopping trip with his adopted mother – Ryan affects a *Die Hard* delinquency. He continues to sport a white tank that frames his leather choker, reaffirming his outsider status in a group of jocks defined within *The O.C.* social strata by their Abercrombie & Fitch habits.

Seth, cast as the self-deprecating stereotype nerd, dons graphic T-shirts by a local Huntington Beach brand, Paul Frank. Worn with Chuck Taylors – an elite basketball shoe – and skinny Levi's, Seth also favours classic fitted polo shirts by Penguin partnered with brown needlecord trousers.

The female protagonists are seen in a mix of high–low fashion, teaming Chanel handbags (due to a limited costume budget, many of Marissa's logoed bags were imitations in the earlier seasons) with garments from the sample sales of local designers. These are worn with flip-flops and form-fitting, layered Lacoste polos. Midriff-baring crop tops and miniskirts or jeans with kitten heels or pointed flats form the template for the girl teen uniform.

The series obeys the conventions of teen dramas, supporting the narrative with telling costume signifiers, albeit with a self-referencing humour and wit. Accelerated plotting, combative boys and teasing, flirtatious girls are offset with darker elements such as dysfunctional parents, drug and alcohol abuse, amid faint parables of rejection and redemption.

above As the daughters, Marissa and Summer, aspire to a mature sophistication so – inversely – the mothers, Julie (Melinda Clarke, third right) and Kirsten (far right), are anxious to appear as youthful as possible. The two generations of the cast are made indistinguishable in age by their universal adoption of similar curvy silhouettes with plunging variants on halter-necked lingerie-like dresses. They are *soigné* evening confections of luxury fabrics; pleated and frilled silk chiffon, silk crêpe de Chine or silk-jersey velvet. Julie luxuriates in advertising both her haute label and her unsubtle *décolletée* with the interlinked double C, bejewelled, logo of Coco Chanel.

above Blair and Dan enter a short-lived relationship which ends when Blair ultimately chooses to be with Chuck. Blair's grown-up groomed look of olive-green cape and mustard-yellow blouse with pussycat bow and matching Hermès Birkin handbag is accessorised with a beanie hat, fishnets and platform patent burgundy heels, providing a sharp contrast to Dan's laid-back skinny jeans and navy peacoat, outfits expressive of their respective emotional and cultural preoccupations.

opposite Referencing the movie *Belle de jour* (1967), starring Catherine Deneuve, showcasing Yves Saint Laurent, the first two episodes of the fourth season see Blair and Serena in Paris as *belles de jour* (beauties of the day). Blair wears a Moschino outsize-print bubble skirt and claims the prestigious Right Bank – home to Dior, Chanel, Lanvin and Louis Vuitton – for herself, while Serena prefers the avant-garde Left Bank in a birdcage dress by George Chakra styled down with an outsize blazer and flats.

GOSSIP GIRL
ERIC DAMAN (2007–2012)

Beginning with a sweeping overview of New York, the teen drama series *Gossip Girl* places the characters firmly in the context of that glamorous and sophisticated arena. Based on the novel series of the same name written by Cecily von Ziegesar, *Gossip Girl* was developed for TV by Josh Schwartz and Stephanie Savage and features a group of privileged adolescents living in Manhattan's Upper East Side. It is intentionally presented as a living fashion magazine, and costume designer Eric Daman deliberately curates recognisable brands on the screen for an eager and aspiring teenage audience:

> 'What I really love about costumes and doing all this, is that you really get to create these characters and these emotions and develop who they are through what we see them wearing. It comes out on display.'

US high-end labels such as Proenza Schouler and Rodarte are combined with couture labels such as Chanel, Dior, Valentino, Balmain, Oscar de la Renta, Jenny Packham, Salvatore Ferragamo, Moschino, Marc Jacobs, Christian Louboutin and Roger Vivier throughout. The plot is subservient to the clothes on view: parties, school dances, debutante balls, modelling shoots, shopping excursions, sleepovers and all social interactions are predicated on the choice of outfit by the protagonists in the drama. The two leading characters are allocated diverse styles. Model Kate Moss provides the inspiration for the laid-back bohemian style of

above Best friends Blair and Serena wear their customised school uniform with loosened collar and tie,
accessorised by Blair with the ever-present embellished
headband – never wearing the same one twice in all
the six seasons. It provides her with a final narcissistic
moment at the mirror – a finishing touch – before she
leaves the house.

opposite left Channelling the sartorial extravagance
of the 1960s British Mod look, Chuck dons a variety of
formal business attire by Paul Stuart and Savile Row's
Ozwald Boateng as the character leans in towards
his professional destiny. These are offset, however, by
his dandyesque personal touches – the pale grey, chalk-
stripe suit, with its narrowly cut jacket sporting skinny
reveres, is partnered with a Bengal-stripe shirt with a
contrast white collar. Jenny is also in Mod mode with
her miniskirt but renders her look contemporary
with pointed stilettos.

opposite centre Earning the approval of André Leon
Talley, then former creative editor of *Vogue*, Serena
confidently walks the runway for Waldorf Designs, the
fashion brand led by Blair's mother Eleanor (Margaret
Colin), who has included in her range a dress designed
by Jenny, the style of which references the puffball
silhouette made popular by the Parisian couturier
Christian Lacroix in the 1980s.

opposite right After initially attempting to copy Blair's
super-groomed, upmarket look and aspiring to be a
fashion designer, Jenny turns punk-rock chick as she
stands her ground in silver cut-out ankle boots, classic
leather jacket and fishnet tights layered beneath
tailored shorts. The goth look is completed with black
T-shirts and multiple necklaces. She carries a studded,
lipstick-red tote.

Serena van der Woodsen (Blake Lively). Whereas Blair Waldorf (Leighton Meester) aspires to screen icon Audrey Hepburn's classic couture.

The group's various interactions in the series are recorded by an unseen narrator following the return of Serena from an unknown destination to her prestigious private school, the Constance Billard School for Girls. All the teenage archetypes are in place. Bad boy Chuck Bass (Ed Westwick), memorably tells Dan Humphrey (Penn Badgley): 'What we're entitled to is a trust fund, maybe a house in the Hamptons, a prescription-drug problem... but happiness does not seem to be on the menu.'

Serena is the insouciant lead, Blair the bitch and Dan the creative oddball with clothes to match – skinny jeans, Henley vests and check shirts. He is based in Brooklyn with his sister Jenny (Taylor Momsen), who is an aspiring Blair, and Nate Archibald (Chace Crawford), the all-round chisel-featured preppy in Ralph Lauren and Brooks Brothers shirts. As a group, they are entitled, narcissistic, not re-motely politically engaged and obsessed with the blog that records their every move. As the series progress, alliances shift, characters develop and relationships flounder or

flourish according to various plot devices. Parents play their part, mostly as an adjunct to their offspring with the exception of Serena's mother Lily (Kelly Rutherford) whose fashion choices offer a contrast to the branded clothes of the teenage cast. Her style of luxurious fabrics, pared-down silhouette and neutral colours such as camel and taupe reference the style of the 1990s fashion icon Carolyn Bessette-Kennedy, who was renowned for her minimal chic and cool blonde looks.

A reboot of *Gossip Girl* appeared in 2021. While set in the same community and retaining the voice of Kristen Bell as narrator, this series focuses on a new cast of characters from a more diverse and contemporary perspective.

NORMAL PEOPLE

LORNA MARIE MUGAN (2020)

Normal People charts the on/off relationship between two teenagers, from schooldays in Sligo, rural Ireland, to post-university Dublin. Sally Rooney's best-selling novel was transferred to the small screen by the author, together with Alice Birch and is an intimate portrayal of all the embarrassments, miscommunications and failed expectations of first love.

Marianne Sheridan (Daisy Edgar-Jones) is the outsider at school, daughter of a wealthy family, Connell Waldron (Paul Mescal) is the high-achieving football player living with his single mother, who works as a cleaner for Marianne's mother. Mutually attracted, their physical relationship is hidden from their peers by Connell — a decision that Marianne finds hurtful, resulting in her ending their connection. Insecure, she feels the denial most painfully. Her vulnerable family background — an abusive deceased father and a cold-hearted mother who seems powerless to protect her from the physical and emotional abuse of her older brother — leaves Marianne lacking in confidence and unsure of her appearance. While the other girls at school wear high-street fashion, Marianne adopts worn jeans, faded dungarees and easy, loose sweaters that allow her to disappear into the background and disguise her body. However, once she embarks on student life at Trinity College, Dublin, she finds her style *métier*. Clever with make-up, hair worn loose with her heavy, sharply cut fringe and a wardrobe of

above 'I went to college and got pretty,' declares Marianne when she re-encounters Connell at university. At liberty away from Sligo and adept at crafting 'smoky eyes', she appears confident in the evolving personal style she has adopted — witness her sophisticated choice of a cream vintage blouse featuring a deep neckline and frilled cuffs. Clearly enjoying her new-found fashion awareness and the respect she gains on campus, she adds a printed silk scarf, casually knotted at the front and a single silver statement earring.

opposite Marianne is comforted by Connell on a visit to the 'ghost' house — an abandoned building at the back of the school — where he apologises for not protecting her from the taunts and bullying of the other pupils. Clever sizing and construction are deployed by the costume designer to create school uniforms that look authentically adolescent on the adult bodies of the cast. The choice of a monastic grey variant of school uniform creates a neutral starting point for the path of their later social evolution, and confirms them as peers academically, if not economically.

vintage print dresses and velvet coats, she becomes the centre of a popular group of students.

In addressing the costume project, designer Lorna Marie Mugan initially spent time on the Trinity College campus taking photographs before creating numerous mood boards. Mugan outlines the tactics she embraces:

'Producing good costumes is a collaborative process; you can't physically do it all by yourself. So, trust in other people's skills is crucial. Each new script can be approached with an adrenaline rush of excitement for the unknown and an equally big fear of failure! That's what keeps it challenging and fun.'

To communicate in visual terms the steps of Marianne's personal growth, from awkward school girl to blossoming student, her wardrobe was rendered authentic by being sourced from popular student outlets in Dublin's vintage shops. These included Harlequin for velvet blazers, blouses from charity shop NCBI in Rathmines and dresses from Jenny Vander.

Connell, though academically brilliant, is out of his depth socially; it is his turn to disappear among the crowd in faded T-shirts and jeans. A liaison of insatiable co-dependence follows with Connell's indecision and emotional withdrawal fracturing their connection repeatedly.

Both seek relationships elsewhere. Rebounding from the tender consent-based sex she enjoys with Connell, Marianne embarks on a series of BDSM trysts, marked by her enveloping herself in victim black. Connell half-heartedly engages with a medical student while consistently ruining his chances of a future with Marianne. The two finally come together again and achieve a level of emotional equilibrium before Connell is offered a place at a university in New York to study creative writing. Even while confessing their love for each other they decide to part, Connell to move to the United States and Marianne to stay in Dublin.

top right Distraught on learning of Marianne's new relationship with the manipulative and controlling Jamie (Fionn O'Shea), Connell walks away from their meeting. Throughout the drama, his sombre-toned wardrobe is that of an introverted, athletic thinker; it is consistently low-key, focusing on an unadorned, brown-leather bomber jacket, a Henley top, Adidas trainers, Gaelic Athletic Association shorts and track bottoms. All worn with a cheap, unadorned, silver chain necklace – an item that at the time of the broadcast had its own Instagram account garnering more than 152,000 followers.

below right Having met up with a group of friends at her parent's Italian villa in Trieste, Marianne and Connell take their cycles into the nearest town. Her style has once again evolved: more relaxed in the summer sun, she is make-up free with her hair loose. Chosen for its impact against the bright Mediterranean light, Marianne's black dress features a favoured holiday silhouette: a marked waistline, fitted bodice with narrow frills, a fit-and-flared skirt and a tightly ruched or pleated bodice with shoulder straps.

opposite At the birthday pool-party, Marianne and Connell are together but distant, she even remarks that Connell never shows her any public display of affection. Although uninhibited in their private life and at leisure in the midst of a familiar social group, she continues to be insecure about her physical attractiveness, particularly when she sees how at ease her contemporaries are in their bikinis. Marianne remains concealed in her old-fashioned, one-piece, black swimsuit beneath a 1930s-inspired floral-print kimono.

above Troy performs his hip-hop routine with Joelle Brooks (Ashley Blaine Featherson-Jenkins). The Kangol bucket hat has been an obligatory accessory for hip-hop artists, alongside loose-fitting, low-slung jeans worn without a belt to expose the waistband of the boxer shorts beneath. This gangsta overtone refers directly to prison workwear, where belts were forbidden and sizing was deemed irrelevant. Heavy gold chains were known as 'donkey' or 'Cuban' chains, made up of thick braided links, usually with the addition of a medallion or cross. Joelle wears a do-rag, a close fitting scarf tied around the back of the head with the ends left loose.

opposite Sam and her co-host Joelle are appalled on entering the radio studio to find a group of right-wing students have taken over the airwaves with their pro-gramme. Subsequently, Sam is targeted by the alt-right, an organisation loosely connected to the far-right white nationalist movement, characterised by the heavy use of social media. The pair assert their African American credentials in their appearance: Sam in Bantu updo and Joelle in long Senegalese twists, while their heavy jewellery includes turquoise, 'the stone of evolution'. Sam's bag and jeans read of *bògòlanfini* (a Malian mud cloth) designs and Joelle's blouse is an African wax print in ochre tones.

DEAR WHITE PEOPLE
CECI (2017–2021)

A spin-off of Justin Simien's award-winning feature film *Dear White People* (2014), the drama is set in the fictional Ivy League college of Winchester University, where Black students are in the minority on campus. It sets out to challenge the endemic racial ine-quality in the US college system while delving into issues such as white privilege, institutional post-racist racism, police brutality, reverse racism, Black beauty and interra-cial dating. The complexities of Black college students facing cultural issues are explored through a cast of diverse characters and situations.

Costume designer Ceci (who professionally opts to go by her first name) specialises in characters that encompass the multidimensionality of young, middle-class Black Americans. She affirms:

'[B]lack people aren't just this one group, we're diverse. We're eclectic. We're militant. We're conservative.'

Throughout the series all pattern is symbolic. Indigenous African prints such as the Ghanaian *kente* cloth – Africa's best-known textile – the Kenyan *kanga* and the Nigerian *aso oke* are contextualised among 1990s-inspired street style of printed Lycra leggings, studded and ripped denim, mohair knitwear and statement jewellery.

The plot of the first season is driven by the Halloween 'blackface' party organised by *Pastiche*, the satirical

Winchester student magazine run by white students, a story broken by Lionel Higgins (DeRon Horton), an aspiring journalist on the college newspaper, *The Independent*, whose personal growth to self expression forms a narrative and visual thread in the series. The repercussions of the party resonate over the seasons as each episode focuses on the perspective of individual characters.

Samantha 'Sam' White (Logan Browning), a biracial student activist who runs her own radio show – the titular *Dear White People* – exposes white privilege and micro-aggressions. Sam externalises her activism through Afrocentric signifiers in her appearance: her hair varying between skinny dreadlocks and Senegalese braids to Bantu-esque updos, heavy silver earrings and breastplate necklaces. Meanwhile, she is dating fellow student, Gabe Mitchell (John Patrick Amedori), who is white, much to the initial resentment of her peers. Troy Fairbanks (Brandon P. Bell), the son of the school's dean, runs successfully for student president until he becomes disillusioned by being manipulated by his father. This trajectory is reflected in his

move away from an English-accented preppy wardrobe. Sam's former friend Colandrea 'Coco' Conners (Antoinette Robertson) is from a Chicago inner-city school and is the first member of her family to go to college. She tries to play down her ethnicity with straight hair and an assimilated wardrobe, initially joining a white sorority in a desire to 'manage her Blackness'. Reggie Green (Marque Richardson), the son of a Black Panther, is involved in a fight at a campus-house party. A gun is drawn on him by a security guard who assumed he was the aggressor, misreading Reggie's 'combative' Afro hair, leather combat gilet and heavy necklace.

The protagonists all live in the Armstrong-Parker 'AP' House, which hosts various groups of Black students. However, under pressure from local benefactors the Hancock family, the university administration decides that the house must integrate, thus limiting spaces for racial solidarity. Throughout the drama, big issues are intertwined with the small, intimate ones of personal relationships as the protagonists engage in cultural and political activism.

top right Chemically straightened hair and wigs for women were first derided in the 1960s with the launch of the Civil Rights Movement (1955–1968) and the desire for authenticity in people of colour. Although Black Panthers and student radicals wore the Afro, ironically the style came to be perceived as too American. Headwraps and bow toppers are Creole antebellum signifiers – Joelle and Sam are adorned in a flash of *bògòlanfini* (Malian mud cloth) atop combative workwear. For Lionel (centre), his blazer and regimental ties conflicts with his full Afro; dropping this style becomes a right of passage as he comes to terms with his homosexuality.

centre right Referred to as the 'Che Guevera' at Fashion Week, Reggie expresses his activist background in his military-style clothing of leather-yoked gilet and combat boots worn with an outsize ivory-bead necklace. Joelle wears a striped coat with twill figuring drawn from the Dorze tribal textiles of Ethiopia. Her complex braided updo is one of many inspired by African styles. Cornrows, braids and dreadlocks are adopted by most of the female cast members of the series with the exception of Coco, who continues to wear a straight wig.

below right Coco and Evangeline (Bola Koleosho) perform a dance in spray-on spandex during a parody of reality show *Big Brother* (2000–) called *Big House – Big Brother* had never been won by an African American woman. The effect of the extreme spandex two-piece is to highlight the sought-after distinction of a 'waist-thin, big ass' physique. Keenly competitive, Coco compromises her conscience by presenting herself as a victim of her background as a poor Black woman from the South Side of Chicago who had an abortion.

opposite The group of young, urban-elite students explore strategies to cope with identity politics, seeking to express their individuality and solidarity through a diversity of style references: ironic preppy pastels, loose Libyan linens, African weaves, prints and jewellery, a Creole wax-print bow topper and a body-con dress.

above When Moordale Secondary School's new head implements a dress code Maeve has to discard her bad-girl alt-uniform of torn fishnets, black leather and combat boots for the new school uniform of blazer and check pleated skirt worn with ribbed hockey socks. Almost a parody of the US traditional high-school uniform, the blazer features exaggerated notched lapels, the edges bound in a wide, contrasting grosgrain ribbon. A striped satin bow at the neck is an additional flourish.

opposite Jean's first appearance on screen is in a rigidly tailored body-con teal-coloured jumpsuit, but as the series advances she turns to a softer silhouette, utilising draped and feminine dresses that acknowledge her body shape in a sensuous but non-suggestive manner. Here, she raises an insouciant glass wearing a belted jersey dress posing in front of a suggestive print of a many-leaved corn husk. The overall production design is linked tightly to costume selection to preserve coherent exposition of character.

SEX EDUCATION
ROSA DIAS (2019–)

S aturated in tones of tangerine and teal, *Sex Education* has all the visual ebullience of a cartoon, while being rooted in the very real concerns of adolescents navigating their way through the complexities of dawning self-realisation. Interracial and LGBTQ+ relationships are a given, normalised throughout the series in both romantic and social settings. Issues such as masturbation, sexual harassment, abortion, parental failure, safe sex and mental health are interrogated in a way that is relatable to the core audience of young adults. There is a nod towards the nostalgia of US high-school movies such as *Breakfast Club* (1985) and *Pretty in Pink* (1986) in the choice of location and fashion inspiration. The fictitious Moordale Secondary School is more like an Ivy League college than a British comprehensive school. Unlike various US high-school series, the drama does not attempt to be fashion-led.

Costume designer, South African-born Rosa Dias, was eager to create a world in which the fashions were non-specific to both time and place but one that prompted a sense of nostalgia too:

> 'Nostalgia is a very personal thing. It relates to age, culture, and how you've been brought up. It was tricky to work out how we could create the concept of nostalgia and make it work all over the world.'

Different eras supply various trends; the 1970s are represented with polychromatic stripes in effervescent

top left Eric's position as emphatically out is mediated though the aesthetic of a West African immigrant family, with a clear acknowledgement of his Nigerian roots. After an attack upon him when in full denim *diamanté* drag, he takes to donning a mid-brown top and trousers – until he recognises that he has to be true to himself. Transfigured, he subsequently appears bathed in cerise light at a party in a steepling headwrap that crowns a body-skimming suit, each element in a different traditional Nigerian print.

centre left Albeit a reluctant school jock, Jackson Marchetti (Kedar Williams-Stirling) happily adopts a maroon and orange letterman or college baseball jacket. The letterman jacket derives its name from the sturdy team sweaters once worn by nineteenth-century college athletes at Harvard that were emblazoned in the middle of the chest with the college's 'H' initial. This garment, emblematic of athletic achievement, became the permanent property of only the most illustrious players, conferring on them campus celebrity status. The letterman sweater developed into the letterman cardigan with an offset letter and it duly evolved into a woollen blouson jacket, embroidered on the left side, normally with leather sleeves and knitted cuffs – the whole suggestive of engagement with baseball and youthful sport in general.

below left Lily Iglehart (Tanya Reynolds, left) and Ola Nyman (Patricia Allison) at the funfair, are friends who became lovers. Lily's quirky character is reflected in the layered colours and textures of her outfit; no stripe is left straight and even the polychrome bumbag plaid is star-crossed. Her lemon-coloured turtleneck sweater is worn beneath a voluminous, soft-peach shirt constricted contrarily by a tube of chevron rack-knit stripes. Ola's signage is relatively understated. Her vintage bottle-green bomber is embroidered with a thumb-sized rainbow symbol, the black fur collar combines with her fade-shaved, natural hair, undercut style to frame her neat features.

opposite Throughout the series, Otis (right) is constantly shown in his three-toned, straight-banded, colour-block jacket. Eric's more extrovert character and his increasing appetite for flamboyant fashion are evident in his silk bomber jacket. The large-scale Picasso imagery rendered in rainbow fairground colours and applied to a standard-build bomber is an indication that the jacket originates from the bespoke services of a digital print-to-product bureau. In an era of mass-customisation, the economy and timeliness of build-of-one production is of great utility to costume designers. Almost camouflaged against the vibrant backdrop of the funfair, the friends discuss the nuances of the relationship between Otis and Maeve.

space-dyed yarns, juxtaposed with vibrant floral prints, textured tank tops and check shirts. Throughout the series, the clothes are accessible to its teenage audience, with many of them to be found on internet sites such as ASOS or high-street clothing stores including AllSaints and Zara.

The leading character is Otis Milburn (Asa Butterfield), socially awkward and burdened with a controlling single mother, Jean (Gillian Anderson), who works as a sex therapist and is overly interested in her son's sex life. The close relationship between the two is exemplified by their clothes: in the initial series both are framed on the sofa, wearing colour-coordinated outfits of teal with an accent of orange.

Surrounded at home by his mother's professional impedimenta, Otis decides to use his insider knowledge to initiate an underground sex-therapy clinic to deal with his classmates' problems He is joined in the venture by Maeve Wiley (Emma Mackey), whose rebellious nature and troubled past are telegraphed by her combination of punk-inspired fishnets and leather jackets.

The two are supported by best friend Eric Effiong (Ncuti Gatwa). Happy with his elective gender as a young gay man, he acts as the lead in idiosyncratic dressing for the series. With pieces culled from high-street labels such as H&M and streetwear brand Lazy Oaf, he holds to a strong bright palette on colour-blocked trousers, checks and floral prints to create his extravagant fashion identity.

CRIME

Costumes designed for the crime genre are not always driven by the characters, but by the crime; they may be devised to intimidate, project malevolence or threaten but most particularly are used as disguise, a misleading indicator of identity. Hooded crimson jumpsuits – the colour of blood and danger – are integral to the plot of Spanish series *La casa de papel* (*Money Heist*, see p 98). They are worn throughout the series to provide anonymity to the criminals and used to confuse those who combat them; both victims and perpetrators are dressed alike – the former under duress – hidden behind an accompanying mask, a caricature of the face of Spanish Surrealist artist, Salvador Dalí. So striking are the ensembles that both the suit and mask continue to be adopted by various left-wing activists and demonstrators – or,

indeed, by cosplay enthusiasts who visited the short-lived immersive show 'Money Heist: The Experience' (2022) held in London.

Clothes can also be used to deflect attention from a crime or to disarm the victim, as Villanelle (Jodie Comer) does in *Killing Eve* (see p 100) with her idiosyncratic fashion choices. Sally Woodward Gentle, executive producer at Sid Gentle Films, told the costume designers on the series that she wanted to avoid the stereotypical male fantasy version of the female killer as being dark and dangerous. In the French series *Lupin* (see p 106), Assane Diop (Omar Sy) is a good guy, but he appears threatening as he swaggers through the streets of Paris in his long, heavy coat inviting comparisons with the classic vampire silhouette, as worn by Bela Lugosi as Count Dracula. Product placement is evident in the drama with the hero sporting a variety of covetable Nike trainers.

Fashion is also used in dark dramas to dispel or disperse implications of decadence or debauchery in the plot

above Hired assassin Villanelle in *Killing Eve* is on the run following a stay in hospital after being stabbed by MI5 operative Eve Polastri (Sandra Oh). She wears Pop-art printed pyjamas stolen from a fellow patient, a ten-year-old boy. The disarming effect of the too-small two-piece is at odds with her heartless murder of the boy. The bespoke pyjamas were printed by a digital bureau in Manchester for the show and gained extensive media coverage before eventually being auctioned at Bonhams, London, in aid of a BAFTA charity.

soundtrack, fashion can provide a sophisticated gloss at odds with a drama's squalid or depraved content, such as the nightclub scenes in the German drama *Babylon Berlin* (see p 84).

The British drama *Peaky Blinders* (see p 80) also renders violence glamorous with the brooding beauty of its protagonists and the stylish editing. Visual emphasis is added through perspective when in the first scene Thomas 'Tommy' Shelby (Cillian Murphy) is mounted on a black steed – his eyes hooded in top-lit shadow under a brooding sky – exuding criminal menace. Shelby wears his distinctive three-piece suit in a sombre herringbone tweed, together with a heavy baker boy cap, prompting a revival in both. The drama proved so influential that it led its creator, Steven Knight, to go into partnership with Garrison Tailors on a *Peaky Blinders* clothing line.

The stark violence and the seedy underworld depicted in the glossy biopic, *The Assassination of Gianni Versace* (see p 94), is seen juxtaposed with the sybaritic way of life and haute-luxe wardrobe of the late Italian couture designer, Gianni Versace.

PEAKY BLINDERS

STEPHANIE COLLIE, LORNA MARIE MUGAN,
ALEXANDRA CAULFIELD, ALISON MCCOSH (2013–2022)

above Once Tommy removes his baker boy hat in the first episode of the series, a whole generation of boys and young men among the viewers headed for the barber to ask for the *Peaky Blinders* distinctive undercut hairstyle, which even became the subject of how-to articles in men's magazines. The style originated in interwar Glasgow, and was espoused by the Neds, a gang of petty criminals. A modified version was adopted by the upper classes in the 1920s.

opposite Tommy, in his street uniform of three-piece suit and mid-calf overcoat, meets with the aristocratic horse trainer and brief love interest May Carleton (Charlotte Riley). Her knitted top and skirt belted at the hips typifies the tubular silhouette popular during the mid-1920s. The line is repeated by the loose-fitting, edge-to-edge jacquard-weave patterned coat featuring a deep shawl collar. She carries a ring-mesh bag, mass-produced during this period in Armor mesh, a flat surface formed by four-armed mesh cells linked by rings at each corner.

As a horse picks its way along the cobbles of a Birmingham back street, the rider, charismatic gang boss Thomas 'Tommy' Shelby (Cillian Murphy), is silhouetted by the fires from a factory furnace, an image that provides a mesmerising opening to the historical drama *Peaky Blinders.* So influential are the costumes in the show, designed in series order by Stephanie Collie, Lorna Marie Mugan, Alexandra Caulfield and Alison McCosh, they created a soaring demand for herringbone-tweed three-piece suits, baker boy caps and collarless Henley shirts. A merchandising boom followed, with themed bars, restaurants, tours, parties and weddings. Authenticity was achieved through Collie's extensive research. She says she examined criminal 'mug shots' from the early twentieth century:

> *'You could see everything in so much detail: the cufflinks, the tiepins, the textures... At heart, I think every Englishman wants to wear a suit.'*

Writer Steven Knight was inspired by a real-life criminal gang known by the same name, who reputedly stitched razor blades into the peak of their caps, terrorising the Midlands in the late nineteenth century. The drama marks the rise to power of Tommy, a local bookmaker – then an illegal practice – in a rundown Birmingham after World War I (1914–1918). Damaged by their experiences in the war, Tommy and his brother Arthur (Paul Anderson) return to the

top left Family matriarch and aunt to the Shelby brothers, Polly (Helen McCrory) is a significant and intimidating member of the Peaky Blinders, a role exemplified in her facsimile of a male three-piece suit – fitted to emphasise her overriding sexuality – and worn with a shirt and tie and a version of a trilby hat with a rounded crown and flat brim.

centre left Less dapper than the Peaky Blinders, vicious gang leader Alfie layers a collarless shirt beneath an oversized military greatcoat. Unkempt in appearance, he nevertheless sports an expensive custom-made Italian fedora, a black high-crowned hat with a curved brim known as a Borsalino, first made in Alessandria, Piedmont, Italy, in 1857 and worn by Jews from Eastern Europe for over a century.

below left Michael Gray (Finn Cole), the son of Polly and cousin to the Shelby siblings wears a two-piece lounge suit – available ready-to-wear in the 1930s and worn for all business scenarios – in his role as chief accountant to Shelby Company Limited. He is flanked by his wife Gina (Anya Taylor-Joy) sporting a fashionable red fox-fur collar, a popular accessory in the 1920s and 1930s worn by those women for whom mink was too expensive. To close the collar, the tail was held by a clip in the jaws of the fox, with its four paws allowed to fall free. Polly is subdued in a maroon knitted sweater and matching cardigan, an early form of the twinset.

opposite Hoping to expand their business empire, Arthur (left), John (Joe Cole) and Tommy Shelby drive to London. All wear the famous baker boy six-segmented cap but show subtle differences in the styling of their suits. Tommy wears a matching three-piece suit, cut from a heavy tweed, with pleat-front trousers. Arthur adopts a more dandyish approach with a tie, flat-fronted trousers, and a patterned waistcoat over which hangs a double Albert chain to secure his pocket watch. Men of all classes wore shirts with separate collars, which would be heavily starched and attached to the shirt with a front and back stud to anchor it in place.

city from the trenches and seek control of the Birmingham streets, with the collusion of the local police force.

The Peaky Blinders are continually at war with multiple individuals, rival gangs and institutions, including the Billy Boys Scottish Protestant gang, the London-based Titanic gang, the Ulster Volunteer Force paramilitary group, British Intelligence, the mysterious Angels of Retribution, Jewish gang leader Alfie Solomons (Tom Hardy), the Chinese Triad and the New York mafia. The confrontations lead to scenes of assassinations, unremitting brutality and violent explosions of murder, torture and mayhem.

The Shelby fortunes are made and lost – in the Wall Street Crash of 1929 – and made again. On the way are run-ins with real-life characters such as Winston Churchill (Andy Nyman, Richard McCabe, Neil Maskell) and fascist leader of the Blackshirts Oswald Mosley (Sam Clafin). Shelby's increasing business success and profitable racketeering lead him to a life of superficial respectability with his election as a Labour Member of Parliament. His upward

mobility is marked by his country house and acres, his social trajectory by the increasing quality and style of his clothing. Tommy's tweed suits – made to measure by tailor Keith Watson of London's Savile Row – become crisper and darker in tone and smoother in texture as he does. Nevertheless, his mid-calf coats remain left open to effect the more menacing slo-mo strut and swagger of a gangster.

BABYLON BERLIN

PIERRE-YVES GAYRAUD (2017–)

A total budget of more than €40 million has made the drama series *Babylon Berlin* the most expensive non-English language TV series ever produced. The €6 million devoted solely to the costumes has helped award-winning costume designer Pierre-Yves Gayraud produce an authentic spectacle of Germany during the Weimar Republic (1918–1933). His intuitive and experimental approach is reflected in his research:

> *'I'd been collecting family photo albums from German flea markets since... 2011. I started this collection specifically in Berlin... most of the collection relates to the period of* Babylon Berlin... *It's very interesting because it documents the lives of real people. Of course, we referred to extravagant figures from the twenties and thirties like Anita Berber, Sebastian Droste, Margo Lion, Marcellus Schiffer, Harald Kreutzberg and Lieselotte Friedlaender.'*

Adapted from the crime novels of Volker Kutscher, and under the direction of Tom Tykwer, Achim von Borries and Henk Handloegten, the series is ambitious in its scope and intentions. The drama is a convincing recreation of the period when the country is still reeling from the effects of World War I, with hyperinflation rife as a result of the stock-market crash of 1929. Germany is on the verge of National Socialism and the subsequent rise to power of Adolf Hitler's Nazi Party. Poverty is extreme, food is scarce

above Gereon's landlady Elisabeth Behnke (Fritzi Haberlandt) has only a small pension but she is able to maintain a level of respectability required by her status. As a widow, she is dressed all in black and wears faded and worn clothes that have been in her wardrobe since before World War I. However, she maintains standards by carrying a polished, although cracked and worn, leather handbag with matching black gloves and hat.

opposite Gereon pauses on the streets of Berlin. Unlike the more formal attire of his colleagues – dark or serge pinstripe suits – he wears a brown three-piece tweed suit with a soft-collared shirt beneath a gaberdine overcoat that marks him out as a newcomer to the capital city. Something of a dandy, his trilby hat with the customary fixed brim angled down at the front is arranged at an insouciant tilt. Both men and women habitually wear hats outdoors, signifying respectability, the women wearing close-fitting cloche hats over bobbed or shingled hair.

previous Unconcerned, and dancing to the rhythm of the music at the Moka Efti nightclub, the flappers – young women who relish the freedom from ladylike restraints – wear uncorseted low-waisted sleeveless tubular dresses known as 'chemises', creating the desirable *la garçonne* boyish look. The impoverished Charlotte (centre) is able to access the nightclub's wardrobe for herself.

top left In a scene resonating with the sound of a hundreds of dancing feet and undercut with flashing images of shimmering sequins, visitors to the Moka Efti disrupt traditional male–female gender roles by utilising furs, feathered headdresses, helmets, headbands, masks and extreme *maquillage* to create a colourful masquerade of costume and fantasy.

below left The fluidity of gender identity was a visually potent element of the 'divine decadence' of 1930s Berlin. Deviating from rigidly defined sex roles and gender, the possibilities of bisexuality were symbolically maintained through cross-dressing. With the accoutrements of femininity – a lavishly embroidered and embellished tunic, adorned with jewellery and draped in a feather boa – an erotic metamorphosis takes place in the Art Deco interior, one observed by an appreciative audience including a man in traditional male dress comprising a commonplace sleeveless knitted jumper, shirt and tie.

opposite Wearing black boots and jodhpurs in this iconic scene, the transvestite Russian Countess Svetlana Sorokina (Severija Janušauskaitė) performs to '*Zu Asche, zu Staub*' (To Ashes, To Dust). At the height of the jazz age in the mid-1920s, a group of musicians and dancers from Harlem, New York, known as the *La Revue nègre* travelled to Paris with the relatively unknown Josephine Baker as the star, creating a stir that rippled through Europe's nightclubs. Starring in the film, *La folie du jour* (1927), Baker's nearly nude body was clad only in a costume comprising sixteen bananas strung onto a skirt. Alongside the cabaret act performed by Sorokina are a troupe of aspiring Baker lookalikes wearing a facsimile of the dancer's costume.

and clothes hard to come by, patched and mended and handed down over the years, an effect Gayraud was eager to introduce.

Although a dazzling cosmopolitan city, Berlin is on the brink of collapse. In contrast, the jazz age is in full swing in the city's nightclubs as decadence and depravity reign. The fashionable *demi-monde*, painted cross-dressers, semi-naked prostitutes and drunken revellers contrast with the poverty evident in the streets.

Police inspector Gereon Rath (Volker Bruch), a war veteran suffering from post-traumatic stress disorder, kept at bay with hefty doses of morphine, is transferred from Cologne to Berlin to dismantle an extortion ring. At the police station he meets Charlotte Ritter (Liv Lisa Fries), a young girl who was chosen out of many others to work on the staff because she was wearing an almost iridescent, emerald-green cloche hat (made by Berlin milliner Fiona Bennett) – at odds with her shabby overcoat with its be-draggled fur collar – making her a noticeable candidate

among the drab clothes and muted colours of her competi-tors for the post. By day, she catalogues photographs of gruesome murders and by night dances at the Moka Efti, a nightclub run by an Armenian crime boss where she makes extra money as a sex worker. Her relationship with Gereon is nuanced and mutually supportive but their feelings remain largely unspoken, they only lose their emotional inhibitions on the dance floor, as seen in a series of invigor-ating and energetic set pieces in various nightclubs

above Dressed as a middle-class couple living in an affluent suburb of Washington D.C., Soviet spies Philip and Elizabeth are careful to wear unobtrusive clothes – nothing too ostentatious or too shabby – when pursuing their daily lives as travel agents. Clothes in sombre colours enable them to fade into the background. He is in a grey single-breasted coat that is evidently not bespoke as the wide lapels are crudely top-stitched by machine. She is in a simple wrap wool coat with a tie belt.

opposite With a body honed and ready for any eventuality, Elizabeth is prepped for action in a costume representative of the archetypal female protagonist, covert operative and lethal female spy. She wears a zip-fronted black-leather jacket and skintight trousers. Her reflexive responses are rendered automatic and efficient after years of training in her youth in the Soviet Union.

THE AMERICANS

JENNY GERING, KATIE IRISH (2013–2018)

S et at the height of the Cold War (1947–1991) between the United States and the Soviet Union, and following the election of Ronald Reagan as president of the United States, Joe Weisberg's drama series *The Americans* portrays how a seemingly ordinary family living in the suburbs of Washington D.C., Philip (Matthew Rhys) and Elizabeth Jennings (Keri Russell) and their two children, are working as spies for the Soviet KGB. Inculcated in the minutiae of American life from an early age and drawing on their physical and psychological training in the Soviet Union, the couple adapt with varying degrees of conviction to their new lives.

The show's first season begins in 1981, when trends from the 1970s were still mainstream. Costume designer Jenny Gering explains:

'I knew going in that when people heard 1980s they'd automatically think neon, big hair, shoulder pads, and I also knew that was actually not true: 1981 looks much more like the late seventies than what people associate with the 1980s. I knew it would be fun for me to reeducate the viewer to the way that time period actually looked. I'm a huge fan of what was going on in fashion at that time.'

Elizabeth's domestic wardrobe reflects the period with 1970 staples such as Fair Isle tank tops, plaid skirts cut on the bias, denim skirts and Lee jeans with zipped back

top left Soviet spies Philip and Elizabeth work under-cover. They adopt the style of the average married couple living in an affluent Washington suburb, and eschew high fashion for comfortable mid-range sweaters and jeans. At FBI agent Stan Beeman's Thanksgiving party, which is a potentially tense situation in view of their activities, the couple are eager to appear relaxed in their knitwear, Philip in a shawl-collared cardigan, Elizabeth in a chevron-patterned mohair jumper made on a Raschel warp-knitting machine, popular in the late 1970s.

centre left Elizabeth is in disguise to meet with her Russian contact. The authenticity of the Russian and US military uniforms in the series was the remit of costume designer Katie Irish. She initially worked as a shopper for the first season of *The Americans*, and sub-sequently as an assistant designer on the second and third seasons, before becoming lead costume designer for the final three seasons.

below left Instructed to wear sombre clothing for success in the workplace, Elizabeth follows the advice in John T. Molloy's book *The Woman's Dress for Success Book* (1977). She exemplifies 1980s power dressing for a business meeting in a sharp-shouldered tailored suit worn over a crisp white shirt with open reveres. Rarely seen in the early 1970s, black became increasingly popular throughout the following decade.

opposite Philip and Elizabeth are rendered unrecog-nisable in an undercover meeting with William Crandall (Dylan Baker), a prospective Soviet spy conducting the US bioweapons programme. Nothing fades more into the background than a beige blouson – a design originating in 1937 when brothers John and Isaac Miller debuted their G9 jacket under the brand name Baracuta. Philip wears his over a worn-looking intarsia jumper that clings to his padded torso. Elizabeth's ill-fitting coat of cheap fabric features the 1980s emphasis on shoulder detail with the gathered sleeve head.

pockets. Belgian designer Diane von Fürstenberg's iconic wrap dress makes an appearance – it was high fashion in 1973 but, by the early 1980s, the dress was diffused throughout various retails outlets and no longer had a fashion edge. As the series moves on from 1981, the colour palette changes from warm browns, oranges and pinks to the cooler colours of the 1980s. It is a realistic vision of the period that is devoid of any nostalgia or the fashion excesses more usually seen in dramas set during this period.

Unlike the men in the FBI office in their ill-fitting big-shouldered Washington power suits, Philip's cover is to run a travel agency, allowing him to wear 1980s off-duty casual wear: open-necked shirts beneath a cardigan or blazer and an Adidas tracksuit. The couple don a variety of wigs, glasses and, in Philip's case, facial hair, as well as an array of costumes, from seductive vamp – Elizabeth working as a honeytrap in black lace lingerie and blonde wig – to Philip in a normcore outfit of droopy moustache and thinning hair, as they kidnap, assassinate and sexually exploit their victims, steal secret plans and hunt down defectors.

The arrival of a new neighbour, FBI agent Stan Beeman (Noah Emmerich), complicates their lives, particularly as Philip has 'married' Beeman's secretary, Martha Hanson (Alison Wright), and is using her for information from Beeman's workplace. The final scene sees the spies' identities uncovered by Beeman. The two head back to Moscow, without their two teenage children. Their son, Henry (Keidrich Sellati), goes to stay with Stan, and their daughter, Paige (Holly Taylor), steps off the train that is carrying them out of the United States, leaving her parents to continue on alone towards their final destination.

THE ASSASSINATION OF GIANNI VERSACE

LOU EYRICH, ALLISON LEACH (2018)

above In a moment of languid intimacy, Gianni's younger long-term partner, Antonio D'Amico (Ricky Martin), proposes marriage to him as they laze by the palatial pool – a vast exercise in product placement that is fully branded with motifs that draw on the Versace heritage. Antonio wears a loose, untied, white-linen beach robe edged with the Greek key design that is a cryptic, never-ending Versace monogram of interlocking negative space and contrast forms. The robe summons faint echoes of the banded decoration of classical Roman garments, such as the toga.

opposite Tones of Miami pink form a production-design leitmotif within the Versace elements of the drama series. Donatella wears a shocking pink – and less revealing – version of the dress made famous by actor Elizabeth Hurley at the premiere of *Four Weddings and a Funeral* in 1994, which attracted global editorial coverage. The Hurley original, held together by gilt-and-silver kilt pins with a *diamanté* Medusa head, came to be known as 'that dress'. Its plunging neckline, buckled shoulder straps and open sides amounted to an upgraded interpretation of the iconography of punk. It is an enduring manifestation of Versace style and remains one of the most significant dresses of the twentieth century.

The Versace family disavow the accuracy of Maureen Orth's book *Vulgar Favors* (1999), which is taken as the source by Ryan Murphy for his docudrama series, *American Crime Story: The Assassination of Gianni Versace* that explores the murder of the Italian fashion designer in 1997. A key issue for the family is their denial of any previous acquaintance between spree killer, Andrew Cunanan (Darren Criss), and his victim, design supremo Gianni Versace (Édgar Ramírez), whereas Orth reported that Cunanan and Versace had met briefly at a San Francisco nightclub in 1990. Despite the criticism of its factual accuracy, the series does attempt to celebrate the designer's work faithfully.

Costume designers Lou Eyrich, a long-time collaborator with Murphy, and Allison Leach developed a deeper appreciation of the designer's aesthetic by researching Versace's garments and accessories at the FIDM Museum in Los Angeles, home to the Gianni Versace Menswear Archive. Leach recalls:

> 'We were able to look at actual garments you couldn't touch without white gloves. We were able to see the seam work and the detail and... recreate the garments with integrity.'

An obligation to respect public awareness of all things Versace underpinned the quest for authenticity in the costumes for this series, which attempts to capture his hyperbolic signature style. Eyrich was able to source Versace

originals from vendors at the Los Angeles clothing market-place, A Current Affair, as well from vintage stores The Way We Wore in Los Angeles and C Madeleine's in Miami. She also shopped online, scoring finds on eBay and Etsy and recreating others with the assistance of tailor Joanne Mills. Guided by Murphy, Eyrich originated two key garments: Versace's silk bathrobe worn in the opening shots and Cunanan's Speedos – both, importantly, in Miami pink.

Since the fatal outcome is a given from the outset of the drama, the strands of exposition are unravelled in a non-linear time frame. Cunanan's degenerating exploits alternate and contrast with glimpses of Gianni's stellar trajectory, from his boyhood in Reggio Calabria to global celebrity. A teenager in the far south of Italy, surrounded by ancient ruins, Gianni was drawn to Greco-Roman myth, architecture and culture that was made glamorously Tech-nicolor in the Italian movies of the 1950s. Gianni styles his dark-haired young sister, Donatella (Penélope Cruz), as a blonde to be a surrogate Patty Pravo (a 1960s Italian singer) and, later, adopts a meld of their features and tousled hair to humanise the fearsome Medusa of his fabled logo. Gianni is encouraged in his design ambitions by his mother, who has a substantial dressmaking business. During the 1970s, he works to establish his own line in Milan, exploding to suc-cess with his first catwalk show and boutique on Via della Spiga in 1978. Harnessing celebrity marketing on a global stage to his look of conspicuous theatricality, in 1989 he introduces a couture collection, Atelier Versace. In 1992, Gianni invests in transforming a Miami beach mansion into his US home staffed and decorated to sybaritic levels of ostentation. This palatial environment provides a refuge for Gianni's recovery from a rare form of ear cancer in 1995, which in turn emboldens him to come out about his homo-sexuality and HIV status at a time of homophobia, by giving an interview with a magazine aimed at gay readers. There are lurid ironies in his death on the threshold of this gated sanctuary, dressed in luxury linen shorts and Medusa print tee and murdered at the hand of Cunanan in anonymous denim cut-offs, unbranded pink baseball cap and grey sweat T-shirt.

top right The opening of the first episode is shot in the Versace mansion, the Casa Casuarina – later a hotel – on Miami Beach's South Beach. Conveying the utter luxuriousness of Gianni's lifestyle, it is an homage to baroque splendour and exuberant excess. The designer follows his early morning ritual, dressed in a Miami-pink silk robe, unbranded and specified by the producer, Murphy.

centre right Gianni adjusts the collar of the harness modelled by Donatella. Jonathan A. Logan, an expert in making leather garments, worked on the replica harness costume for the series. Sex was the key to Gianni's aesthetic: his bondage collection of autumn/winter 1992 was evidence of the progressively explicit fetish clothing entering the fashion mainstream with its post-punk appropriation of the leather straps and hardware of the female dominatrix. Donatella, directing the younger line Versus (Versace), aimed to project a harder-edged modernity to the collection with her public image of black leather, blonde hair and dark shades. Following on from Versace's collection, the recurring theme of fetish in fashion has become more extreme, regularly moving from the sexual subculture to the catwalk.

below right Throughout his professional life, Gianni attempts to persuade his sister and muse Donatella of her ability to take over from him at his death. Gianni also wants to take the mature company to the stock market, which Donatella resists both before and after his death, maintaining that the Versace company represents his life and legacy. As a compromise, she agrees to oversee Versus (Versace), the more youthful line of the label from 1990. On his death, she took over the design directorship of the main label. Her funeral gown and veil is a ready expression of her emotions and the decorous gothic aspects of Versace style.

opposite In his atelier, Gianni essays one of his designs on the dress stand. The print on the dress is in his preferred colour combination of black and gold. It features his adopted crest, the Medusa's head, which typifies the ancient mythological references commonly featured in his work. The decadent mix of mannered, baroque prints with overt sexiness – dresses slashed to the waist or cut down to the buttock – represent the showy glamour and provocative allure inherent in the Versace label.

THE MONEY HEIST
(LA CASA DE PAPEL)
ROSA SOLANO, CARLOS DÍEZ (2017–2021)

above Veteran Serbian soldier-turned-robber Helsinki (Darko Perić) models his jumpsuit, weaponry and chest rig (a form of tactical gear storage that is mounted on the chest). Protective military-style armour entered mainstream fashion during the twenty-first century with designers appropriating the use of performance textiles such as high-tenacity nylon Kevlar, and engineered hardware to create urban streetwear.

opposite The masks are based on the stylised facial image of the Spanish Surrealist artist Salvador Dalí. Surrealism had its roots in the Dadaist movement whose main purpose was to challenge the social norms of the capitalist state and undermine the status quo. The masks are a device used in the series not only to impede facial recognition, but also to conceal the emotions of the wearer to distance themselves from their victims.

Created by Álex Pina, *The Money Heist (La casa de papel)* is an escapist fable and compelling crime drama that combines the story of a heist with an exploration of the complex romantic and familial relationships of the protagonists. Told with panache, the Spanish series is set in Madrid and concerns an enigmatic man known as 'The Professor' (Álvaro Morte), aka Sergio Marquina/Salvador 'Salva' Martín, who recruits an outcast gang of career criminals to carry out an ambitious plan to print then steal millions of euros in authentic, untraceable cash from the Royal Mint of Spain. He is hopeful that his mantra of 'no bloodshed' throughout the heist and his storming of the money-making machine of the state in a Robin Hood-like attempt to redistribute wealth will endear him to the public, however, he is doomed to disappointment.

The action drama has a political edge: an anti-capitalist stance is invoked whenever the gang's borrowed anthem, the late nineteenth-century Italian protest folk song '*Bella Ciao*', is heard. Costume designer Carlos Díez followed Rosa Solano, who was responsible for the first fifteen episodes of the drama. He admits:

> '*Dressing all the characters individually and as a group, with the iconic red jumpsuits they use in the heist, has been a huge challenge.*'

Red was chosen for the colour of the jumpsuits that disguise the identity of the criminals as it is a colour

above Dressed as the archetypal professor with a loosened tie, tweed coat and spectacles, The Professor (third right) heads his troupe of renegades who have adopted the names of capital cities (left to right): Oslo (Roberto Garcia), Helsinki (Darko Perić), Tokyo (Úrsula Corberó), Denver (Jaime Lorente), Berlin (Pedro Alonso), Nairobi (Alba Flores), Moscow (Paco Tous) and Rio (Miguel Herrán). Tokyo wears the street garb of the outsider – slashed jeans, fingerless gloves and a red bomber jacket – the younger members of the gang, skinny jeans and hoodies.

associated with left-wing politics since the French Revolution (1789–1799) and its subsequent adoption by the Bolsheviks in the Russian Revolution of 1917.

Each season required around 500 of the jumpsuits, with eight required for each character. Díez reconfigured the jumpsuits for the second heist on the Bank of Spain to differentiate between the two events, the former being looser fitting and with fewer details. The later jumpsuits were made in Italy and were more form-fitting, with belts and an adjustable back, new zippers, and underarm vents.

The plot twists in the series are constant, creating an atmosphere of adrenaline-fuelled chaos. The Professor anticipates every move made by the negotiating inspector Raquel Murillo (Itziar Ituño) and her crew, foiling their attempts to infiltrate the bank and safely recover the hostages. The labyrinthine subplots result in many shifting loyalties between the criminals and their victims, with some of the main characters changing sides and other hostages colluding with the criminals for monetary reward.

KILLING EVE

PHOEBE DE GAYE, CHARLOTTE MITCHELL,
SAM PERRY (2018–2022)

above In Barcelona on the way to meet her new keeper, the dangerous Dasha Duzran (Harriet Walter), an ex-Olympic gymnast who was once the KGB's foremost assassin, Villanelle attempts to appear disarming. She wears a floral headband and a deceptively prim and concealing, Victorian-inspired, fitted, floral maxi dress with leg-of-mutton sleeves by The Vampire's Wife, a romantic and gothic British cult label founded by Susie Cave.

opposite Playing the *ingénue* in a Molly Goddard frilled and smocked, shocking-pink tulle dress, Villanelle is challenged by her handler Konstantin (Kin Bodnia) on her suitability to continue as a hired assassin after she has slaughtered not only the original target – a witness to her assassination of a mafia boss – but also five other people.

Taking the epigram 'dressing to kill' literally, the protagonist of the spy thriller *Killing Eve* has the perfect job as a hired assassin. The drama was adapted from Luke Jennings' novels initially by Phoebe Waller-Bridge for the first season and then a new writer for each subsequent season. It follows the mutual fascination between the fashion-obsessive psychopathic killer Villanelle (Jodie Comer) and MI5 agent Eve Polastri (Sandra Oh), who is seemingly happily married and working for UK national security. Where Villanelle projects a general demeanour of wry impassivity – solid in her narcissistic apparel and convictions – her moral adversary Eve reveals an eloquent conflicted angst, set against the blank canvas of a subdued and practical wardrobe.

As the drama and connotations of costume unfold over the course of four seasons, among other aspects the fluidity of Villanelle's wardrobe mirrors the exposition of her appetites. Designed – in season order – by Phoebe De Gaye, Charlotte Mitchell and – from season three – Sam Perry, dress is wordlessly used to underscore the cryptic psychology of the protagonists. As Mitchell records:

'To have the freedom and large budget to design and style Villanelle was a dream, a key word for her at mood-board stage would be "attention seeking" but she isn't always this way, and sometimes as a designer you have to decide when your costumes are

top left On an expedition to Aberdeen, Villanelle and Dasha sign in at the hotel, pretending to be mother and daughter. Always eager to look the part, Villanelle wears an oversize mohair coat with a chain trim running down both the centre front and the outside of the raglan sleeves by Scottish 'post-gender' designer, Charles Jeffrey. Although she describes it as the family tartan, the designer created the tartan for his own label, registered with the Scottish Register of Tartans.

centre left Instructed by the Twelve, an organisation of twelve unseen individuals, to kill Dasha, Villanelle takes her to play golf. Concerned, as ever, to evince maximum impact from the visual eccentricity of her clothes, she wears a plaid, cropped bomber jacket, lavishly festooned in apple-green faux Mongolian lamb. This look, from London label Charlotte Knowles, is teamed with a pair of gargantuan Gucci trousers, replete with heavy pleats. Villanelle derides Dasha for looking like 'a prophylactic that can't play golf' before she bludgeons her to death with a golf club.

below left Feeling ambivalent about her career as an assassin, Villanelle travels to Poland in the hope of reconnecting with her family. Adopting homespun dress in an attempt to fit in with the rural community – a patterned 1970s Paco Rabanne top and a pinafore with a heart-shaped bib – she confronts her mother with fake, bloody tears. Villanelle is disappointed when her mother continues to reject her, so she kills her and sets fire to the house.

opposite Villanelle arrives on Eve's doorstep in a seductively sheer, black chiffon gown with a matching spotted veil by Sarah Burton for Alexander McQueen. She remarks that she has come to kill Eve and is in mourning, 'dressed for the occasion'. Emblematic of their mutual fascination, Villanelle challenges Eve to swallow some pills, which she does, even when Villanelle taunts her that they are poisonous. Only when Eve attempts to make herself vomit does she admit that the pills are harmless.

going to stand out and when they are not. It starts with the script... I was keen that she wouldn't always be provocative in her fashion choices.'
Ebullient and playfully sinister, Villanelle dons bright colours and striking abstract prints in a La DoubleJ midi, printed with a regiment of mandalas, worn above knee-high Golden Goose cowboy boots. Villanelle's otherness is upheld when a voluminous, egg-yellow duster coat by Loewe, trailing long rouleau ties at the collar, is worn in counterpoint to paratrooper boots.

Villanelle is at her most dangerous when she is at her most idiosyncratic, in contrast to Eve who consistently wears drab colours and practical clothes. Eve's layers of clothing are usually crumpled and dishevelled, reflecting the amount of stress she is under.

When Eve connects a number of unexplained killings with Villanelle, she is delighted to abandon the tedium of her security-analyst desk job in order to pursue the professional spree killer, who has previously expressed a desire for 'someone to play with'. Villanelle and Eve become mutually fixated, engendering several life-or-death confrontations where both duly pull back from the brink of terminating their adversary.

THE UNDOING

SIGNE SEJLUND (2020)

above Grace tells Jonathan that the dress code for the fundraiser auction is 'fancy glam'. Privileged beyond imagining – her father is a billionaire – she dons a distinctive couture gown by Parisian couturier Givenchy, a shimmering, light-reflective, metallic pleated dress with plunging neckline.

opposite above Grace is inscrutable. A clinical psychologist with a PhD from Harvard University who acts as a relationship counsellor to Manhattan's elite, she maintains an unwavering commitment to her own faultless personal style. It is represented here in an all-concealing, mid-calf dress with full sleeves, the purple silk deliberately chosen to contrast with her red hair.

opposite below Grace in one of the many coats she wears around the New York streets or to pick up her son from school. There is an haute-hippy aesthetic evident in the textured, full-skirted, fitted mid-calf coat, the shawl collar extending into a slouchy hood. Created by the costume designer, the coat provoked almost as much attention as the actual drama.

Shot on the wintry streets of New York, psychological thriller *The Undoing*, based on the novel *You Should Have Known* (2014) by Jean Hanff Korelitz, provides a chilling insight into the upper echelons of New York's Upper East Side. Produced by David E. Kelly, the miniseries offers an unsettling account of how the members of a wealthy and privileged society respond to the murder of an outsider. With wardrobes curated by costume designer Signe Sejlund – sourced mainly from New York store Bergdorf Goodman – the chilly demeanour of Grace Fraser (Nicole Kidman) is offset by a distinctive use of colour, embracing all shades of purple (mauve, aubergine and lilac) alongside moss green and olive. These are mediated through an elongated silhouette of soft drapey fabrics such as crêpe, silk and velvet, emphasizing her queenly deportment and signifying her place in the privileged society of the Upper East Side. For her de-stressing walks around Manhattan, she wears a series of eye-catching coats including a customised, crimson-red overcoat by high-end retailer Max Mara and a teal, cardigan-style coat from The Row. Sejlund confirms their importance:

> *'I am not afraid to be quite bold, so she's walking around New York constantly, so she needed coats, because that's what you wear when you're in New York. So it became "The Coat Show".'*

Grace only drops her guard when she is with her charmingly raffish British husband Jonathan (Hugh Grant), a paediatric oncologist, and when at home she adopts a series of form-enhancing, luxury silk and cashmere loungewear.

The social life of the New York elite is centred on Reardon, a private school attended by their twelve-year-old son. Grace is a member of the school's all-powerful parents' committee, which reluctantly accepts the young and beautiful mother of a scholarship boy, Elena Alves (Matilda De Angelis), into their inner circle. A fundraiser for the school sets the plot in motion. At the prestigious event held in a luxurious penthouse apartment – there are paintings by David Hockney on the walls – Elena appears to be obsessed by Grace. The next day, Elena is found bludgeoned to death in her studio. Jonathan disappears and Grace is challenged by two NYPD detectives who inform her that Elena was Jonathan's mistress and he is the father of her baby daughter. Jonathan is brought to trial and, while awaiting the verdict, he kidnaps his son and heads for the Canadian border, but he is foiled in his attempt in a car chase conducted from the private helicopter of Grace's wealthy father, Franklin Reinhardt (Donald Sutherland).

above Usually favouring hoodies and sweats, Assane dons a three-piece suit to blend in with the super-rich as he attends the invitation-only auction with a view to buying the necklace. Subject to congratulatory applause, he successfully takes the bidding from €40 million to €60 million in an attempt to keep within the 7-minute time frame required for his partners in crime to effect the scam.

right Assane, his estranged wife Claire (Ludivine Sagnier) and son Raoul (Etan Simon) visit the beach. Raoul wears a classic duffel coat and his mother is quietly underplayed in a pale-grey double-breasted coat and beanie. Assane has abandoned his heavy coat in favour of relatable, accessible brands, including a Barbour waxed jacket over a maroon Fred Perry track top.

above Assane replicates the flourish and swirl of Lupin's long cloak with a dramatic, voluminous ankle-length double-breasted coat with a highwayman collar. Fleet of foot, he wears the classic black, white and red colourway Nike Air Jordan 1 Mid SE Union Black Toes, released in 2020 and inspired by the original Air Jordan 1 Black Toe of 2016.

LUPIN

SOPHIE-CHARLOTTE LARGET,
CAMILLE JANBON (2021–)

Invented by French writer Maurice Leblanc in 1905, Arsène Lupin is a quintessential gentleman thief, sporting a top hat and monocle, the debonair master of disguise executed daring heists and intrepid escapes. In the French TV thriller *Lupin* created by George Kay and François Uzan, Assane Diop (Omar Sy) is given a copy of the collection of Leblanc's stories as a child by his father. He then takes the gentleman burglar (*cambrioleur*) as his role model, redistributing wealth and righting wrongs. *Lupin* follows Assane's audacious plan to steal Queen Marie-Antoinette's necklace, reported lost twenty-five years ago but about to be auctioned at the Louvre.

Costume designers Sophie-Charlotte Larget (ten episodes) and Camille Janbon (seven episodes) render the hero in contemporary garb, abandoning the top hat, monocle and cane for a flat cap and a variety of Nike trainers. Lead actor Sy talked at length to the costume designers about dressing Assane:

'We were aware that the character comes with a rich iconography. We had to create something new while staying true to Lupin's spirit.'

Assane's father Babakar (Fargass Assandé), an immigrant from Senegal hired as a chauffeur by the wealthy white Parisian Hubert Pellegrini (Hervé Pierre), had been framed for the theft of the necklace in an insurance scam twenty-five years previously. He subsequently commited suicide in prison. Determined to clear his father's name, Assane moves, chameleon-like, through Parisian society as he seeks revenge for his father's death, which left him an orphan. Deploying charm, meticulous planning and a series of shapeshifting disguises – facilitated by his colour as the police seem unable to differentiate between one Black person and another – Assane uses illusionist skills and quick-thinking to evade capture, until the spectacular denouement when Hubert is finally bought to justice.

HISTORICAL

Costume drama series, as opposed to dramas that are simply set in the past, demand a difference in approach for the costume designer. One is to do with resplendent spectacle, where the fashions are the main attraction, and the settings and costumes aim to create a sense of romantic nostalgia and a picturesque vision of the past. The other is more concerned with authenticity appropriate to the narrative, where the set and the fashions are replicated as closely as possible to those of a particular era, as with the drama series *The Pursuit of Love* (see p 132), a meticulous recreation of the fashions of the interwar years. Tapping into the perennial urge among fashion designers to reflect the careless leisure of British gentry, it prompted a resurgence in floral-printed tea dresses, pastel cardigans and well-cut tweeds.

The alternative approach in designing for the screen is to opt for a liberal pastiche of the period, where character and intent are subjugated to a playful version of the epoch, as with the raunchy Regency romp, *Bridgerton* (see p 114). So influential is the drama that the British Fashion Council (BFC), in partnership with Netflix,

commissioned three young designers, BFC Scholars Ifeanyl Okwuadi, Latifa Niyazi and Jeongmin Ji, to create looks inspired by the Bridgerton characters and the Regency era. They were mentored by Jenny Packham, who is the favourite designer of Catherine, Princess of Wales. The final pieces were modelled in styled publicity shots by cast members.

Although the costume designer may strive for realism, a period drama inevitably reveals as much about the time in which it is made as the historical period in which it is set. It is a rare historical drama in which female faces are untouched by the application of contemporary cosmetics, or an injudicious use of Botox. Although character actors are allowed to have a compromised grin, the teeth of the leading actors in most dramas set in the past are uniform and white, hence the perfect teeth of the protagonists of *Outlander* (see p 110). On such mundane details authenticity can be derailed.

Created and overseen by Peter Morgan, *The Crown* (see p 134) is a lavish docudrama series, with an overall production budget totalling £250 million. It follows British

above In Julian Fellowes' *The Gilded Age*, Bertha Russell (Carrie Coon), the ambitious wife of the railway tycoon and robber baron George (Morgan Spector) is determined to make an entrance at the ball, descending the staircase to the awaiting guests in a monochrome embroidered gown with a sweeping train. She is delighted that at last the elitist old money of New York, among them Mrs Astor (Donna Murphy), have finally been inveigled into accepting her hospitality.

royalty through the regular episodes of private and public turbulence that surfaced during the reign of Queen Elizabeth II, whose family, in its many complex incarnations have filled more viewfinders than any other in history. For this series, the costume designer has access to innumerable reference images but must draw a fine line between respecting what is already inscribed in the public memory and overindulging creative licence, in order to provide a balance between the two.

In the United States, from 1870 to 1900 unfettered capitalism drew off vast fortunes from the post-Civil War peace dividend, creating a class of ostentatious plutocrats, who became denizens of Fifth Avenue mansions and the public hardcore of New York's high society. This coterie is the focus of the costume drama series *The Gilded Age* (see p 124). However, it is costumed for spectacular impact in the first instance and any true representation based on contemporary research is generically authentic rather than specific to historic individuals.

OUTLANDER

TERRY DRESBACH, TRISHA BIGGAR, NINA AYRES,
GLENNE CAMPBELL (2014–)

above A symbol of Highland identity for many centuries, tartan cloth was originally left untailored as a long rectangular strip of fabric called a plaid, and worn about the shoulders. At some point in the eighteenth century, the plaid was transformed into a kilt. Following the Battle of Culloden, the final Disarming Act of 1746 banned Highland clothing from being worn by men and boys in Scotland in an attempt to suppress the Jacobite cause. The soft woollen cap, worn to one side, is known as a 'bonnet'.

opposite Claire and her eighteenth-century husband Jamie pause for a moment together. Created from indigenous natural dyes, early tweeds and tartans were muted in colour and so blended in with the Scottish landscape. She wears a functional version of the fashions of the period, appropriate to her status, with a small padded roll of cloth tied around the waist beneath a gathered skirt in imitation of the panniered skirt, which in the most formal robes extended several feet sideways beyond the body. The bodice is unadorned, with the stomacher, a stiffened triangular bodice insert, covering the corset. The costumes throughout the series show wear and tear, and are patched and mended for authenticity.

A time-travelling historical epic of swashbuckling romance and fantasy that requires an element of willing suspension of disbelief, *Outlander* is based on a series of books by US author Diana Gabaldon. Following the carnage of World War II (1939–1945) – where she is nursing soldiers at the front – Claire Randall (Caitríona Balfe) holidays in the Scottish Highlands with her husband, Frank (Tobias Menzies). Visiting the stones of Craigh na Dun, she is magically transported back to 1743 where she is rescued from the dastardly intentions of English redcoat Captain Jonathan 'Black Jack' Randall (also played by Menzies), her husband's forbear, by the Highlander Jamie Fraser (Sam Heughan), a young Scottish laird. Although initially desperate to return to her own time and place, the romantic central fulcrum to the drama is the developing relationship between the two as they travel to the court of King Louis XV of France with the intention of plotting to halt the Jacobite rebellion of 1745, knowing it will prove to be a disaster for Scotland.

Spectacular scenery and compelling costumes, initially designed by Terry Dresbach for the first four seasons, followed by Trisha Biggar (twelve episodes), Nina Ayres (nine episodes) and Glenne Campbell (four episodes), are an essential element of the visual experience of the series. Dresbach recalls:

'The biggest challenge in costuming the series was getting as close as possible to the standards of

above After World War II, Claire hopes to rekindle her marriage to her husband Frank, who has been away working as an intelligence officer during the war. The couple return to a village near Inverness for a second honeymoon. Claire's clothes show the military influence on women's fashions still evident in 1945 in the double-breasted, sharp-shouldered coat in navy blue.

authenticity we insanely set for ourselves. For season two, we quickly figured out we were going to have to create most of our own fabrics and accessories. So we set up an embroidery team; we hand-painted fabrics; we made buttons, shoes, bags and hats, as well as petticoats and gloves.'

Dresbach was also confronted with three diverse types of costume as the drama moves through time frames and countries. The homespun tweeds, tartans and knitted garments of eighteenth-century Scotland and the extravagant embellished frills and furbelows at the French court provide contrast to the Boston years in the 1960s, when US First Lady Jacqueline Kennedy exerted her style influence of pared-back minimalism on Claire's contemporary wardrobe.

For Claire's first appearance in the Paris streets in the eighteenth century, Dresbach provides a witty acknowledgement of Christian Dior's New Look of 1947 as she wears a facsimile of Dior's iconic hourglass Bar suit and conical hat. Back in Scotland, believing Jamie to be killed at

top right Claire wears the *robe à la française* for her visit to Versailles where she meets Mary Hawkins (Rosie Day, centre), an ancestor of her contemporary husband Frank. Fashionable during the mid-eighteenth century, the Rococo style of dress dominated the court of King Louis XV. Distinguished by the deep yellow of her robe among the pale green and ecru, Claire's fitted bodice is open at the front to reveal a stomacher with an overskirt that is parted in the front to reveal the petticoat. Trimming and adornment were lavish at court, with France leading the way in silk weaving and embroidery.

below right In Paris in 1774, Jamie wears the male three-piece suit, a combination that dates from the late seventeenth century. Referencing his rural background, and emphasising his Scottish antecedents, his relatively unadorned coat, knee-length waistcoat and breeches are in contrast to the Parisians whose coats are embellished with frogging in gold or silver thread around the front opening, cuffs and the pocket flaps. A frill of lace, or jabot, is fastened around the neck, whereas Jamie wears a simple neckcloth and natural hair, unlike the powdered wigs worn by the others at court.

the Battle of Culloden (1746) and carrying his child, Claire returns to the stones and is transported back to the 1940s and her modern-day husband. Claire's story moves to 1960s Boston where she struggles to adjust to life with Frank while training to be a surgeon and raising Jamie's daughter Brianna (Sophie Skelton).

When Frank is killed in a car crash twenty years later, Claire visits Scotland with her by-then adult daughter and discovers that Jamie was not killed at Culloden but went into hiding. She returns to the eighteenth century and the two are reunited. Their emotional and physical bond becomes even stronger as they suffer various vicissitudes and adventures in the West Indies before building their lives together in the rough and dangerous backcountry of North Carolina, where they help form a settlement at Fraser's Ridge.

above The youngest daughter of Lady Featherington, and the author of a notorious scandal sheet that she writes under the *nom de plume* 'Lady Whistledown', Penelope is customarily dressed in a variety of eye-catching hues enhancing her distinctive red hair. The cap sleeves and neckline of her high-waisted gown are embellished with a floral decoration of cutout *guipure* lace flowers.

BRIDGERTON

ELLEN MIROJNICK, SOPHIE CANALE (2020–)

Rogues, rakes, devilishly handsome dukes and dandies and spirited beautiful débutantes frolic against the visually ravishing backdrop of Regency-era (1811–1820) London in the costume drama *Bridgerton*. Manicured lawns and historic terraces are all bathed in a hyperreal glow of saturated colour, every character is bejewelled, every house festooned with wisteria, every garden filled with roses. Created by Chris Van Dusen and produced by Shonda Rhimes, the series is inspired by US author Julia Quinn's best-selling series of novels.

Bridgerton is set in a period of deeply erotic dress as the Neoclassical mode liberated the female body and the waistline rose high under the breasts, which were supported by stays and very much on display. Men wore close-fitting pantaloons fashioned out of fabric cut on the bias, or knitted jersey in a natural buff colour that mimicked nakedness. They were back-laced to describe a higher tighter fit so as to outline the fork of the body.

In a series renowned for its forthright sexual scenes, costume designers Ellen Mirojnick in the first season and then Sophie Canale in the second are understandably and demonstrably reticent about the scandalous reality of Regency costume – when muslin dresses were dampened down to show every contour of the body. Instead, they aim for a contemporary look rather than for historical accuracy, a decision that proved popular with an audience keen to

above Although accepted by the *ton* high society, the chemise was considered unsuitable for formal court occasions, for which the eighteenth-century *robe à la française* continued to be worn until the era of King George IV. Flat-backed and fronted, the gown became increasingly wide at the hips, projecting up to several feet at each side. A whalebone corset funnels the bodice into an inverted cone shape. Queen Charlotte, the wife of George III, and her courtiers wear enormous and elaborate wigs in the series. At the time of George III, hair was extravagantly dressed with several layers of frizzed rolls and padded out with gauze, a style made popular by the French queen Marie-Antoinette.

right Standing on the steps of the family home is the widowed Viscountess Violet Bridgerton (Ruth Gemmel, top left) and her 'perfectly handsome sons and perfectly beautiful daughters'. Neoclassical fashions from 1780 to 1820 are most closely associated with the *robe en chemise* or *batiste*, a more relaxed style of dress that first appeared in France in the 1780s. The informality of the period is marked by a light palette of pale blues and greens, and softly draped fabrics worn by the three Bridgerton daughters and their mother.

above Lady Featherington (second left) is married to a committed gambler, yet she is ambitious and hopeful of marrying off her daughters (left to right), Penelope, Philippa (Harriet Cains) and Prudence (Bessie Carter) to rich suitors. She adorns them in over-elaborate gowns in bright shades of citrus in an attempt to attract potential suitors. Their eye-catching costumes are in contrast to the more subtle approach adopted by Lady Bridgerton for her daughters, who are clothed in simple silhouettes and pastel hues.

right Simon, the Duke of Hastings, dances with Daphne. He wears a figured brocade waistcoat cut across the waist to emphasize his long legs. His neckwear is complex, originally the cravat would have been used to hold the collar together, rather than it being left open to emphasize the hero's rakishness, with the cravat worn beneath.

opposite Antony (left) and his friend, the Duke of Hastings, are dressed as the archetypal dandies of the Regency period, which extolled the virtues of a body contoured by expert tailoring. They both wear double-breasted coats cut from wool broadcloth moulded to the shoulders and cut high on the waist, worn with pantaloons, a cross between breeches and trousers.

replicate the corseted femininity of the period, confirmed by Mirojnick:

> 'This was not going to be like a Jane Austen adaptation. How could we shift the aesthetics of a period drama to make it feel scandalous and modern?'

Set in London in 1813, when the Regent reigned in place of King George III, the drama opens as the daughters of two households are preparing for their presentation at court. Described as 'faultless' by Queen Charlotte (Golda Rosheuvel) when she is presented at court, Daphne Bridgerton (Phoebe Dynevor) secures her place in the *ton*, the fashionable and much envied upper echelons of society. Joining her are the daughters of the impecunious but equally aspirational neighbour, Lady Portia Featherington (Polly Walker), which sets the stage for ambitious mothers, scheming rivals and fortune hunters. The eldest son of the Dowager Viscountess Bridgerton, Lord Anthony (Jonathan Bailey), attempts to marry Daphne off to a suitably aristocratic but unattractive and morally reprehensible suitor. Horrified, she makes a pact with the newly arrived and sought-after Simon Basset (Regé-Jean Page), the handsome Duke of Hastings, to a pretend romance, as he too is besieged by matchmaking mamas. All

is happily resolved by the final ball of the first season. Like a Georgian-era *Gossip Girl* (see p 62), every sexual peccadillo is noted by the anonymous narrator of a scandal sheet written by the mysterious Lady Whistledown (voiced by Julie Andrews), who proves to be the *nom de plume* of the youngest Featherington daughter, Penelope (Nicola Coughlan).

above Prompted by the Napoleonic Wars (1803-1815) between France and England, military detailing influenced men's and women's fashions. Lister eagerly adopts a short and extremely tight-fitting jacket known as a 'pelisse' – a garment mentioned in her diaries – that adheres to the lines of the uniform of the hussars. Sometimes known as a 'spencer' jacket in women's riding attire, it was decorated with parallel rows of frogging and three rows of buttons, and echoes of the multi-caped sleeves of men's riding dress.

opposite Armed with a silver-topped cane for potential door rapping, Lister strides out to take over the role of rent collector from her dying manager. With a swagger, she takes to the streets of Shibden in an ankle-length full-skirted version of a man's frock coat, which the costume designer based on an original coat from the 1830s. There is a degree of fluidity in the terminology applied to menswear and womenswear versions of this cut, from 'frock coat' to 'greatcoat' and the French '*redingote*'. Popular since the beginning of the nineteenth century, it was customarily worn without a jacket over a waistcoat and shirt. The coat is fitted to the body with a horizontal seam at the waist.

GENTLEMAN JACK

TOM PYE (2019–)

Anne Lister, an upper-class landowner and industrialist of the nineteenth century who obsessively detailed her lesbian affairs in a five-million word diary, part of which was written in a secret code, is the subject of *Gentleman Jack*, a romantic drama created and written by Sally Wainwright. The opening sequence of the series features Anne (Suranne Jones) getting dressed in a combination of female clothing – a back-laced corset with a decorated wooden busk placed between her breasts – and male drawers and certain paraphernalia largely assigned to masculinity. The fob watch, cravat and top hat are all potential, if ambiguous, signifiers of her sexual orientation.

When dressed in a sombre business-like manner, her transgression is limited to minor infringements of the fine line between men's formal outdoor attire and the aristocratic female riding habit of that era, which are residually evidenced in dressage to this day. Anne, with a large country estate, was undoubtedly an expert equestrian. When she sports a walking cane, it is a surrogate riding crop; her top hat – its brim bridged gently aloft to accommodate rouleaux side curls – is a woman's riding hat with a profile subtly distinct from the taller and straighter male version. Her orientation towards black and flannel grey is subversive only in its distance from the standard formulae of feminine representation.

above Here, the couple pose as if for a family portrait. Lister, with tight chignon, stands erect and dominant in high-collared white shirt, wrapped stock and charcoal vest, contrasted to Walker's timidity and vulnerability – emphasized by her froth of tight curls and by sensitive pastel hues, the delicate chintz prints and volumes of ruching, gathers and pleats. Fashions of the Romantic era offer an idealised view of country life that incorporates floral-sprigged cottons, straw bonnets, baskets and parasols. By the 1830s, many advances had been made in printing techniques, which led to a fashion for simple, printed cotton fabrics featuring small-scale floral designs.

Set between 1832 to 1834, the drama features a period in fashion, shortly before Queen Victoria ascended the throne, that provided a bridge between the columnar high-waisted Empire-line dress of the Georgian era and the full-blown crinoline which reached its apogee in 1859. The transition was marked by the fashions of the Romantic era, a period researched by costume designer Tom Pye, a veteran of both Broadway and West End productions, as well as a designer for opera and ballet:

> 'I realised how much Anne was kind of a chameleon – she had her life on the estate, but she also hobnobbed around with a lot of aristocracy and court. So there were a lot of ex-girlfriends and friends that were all very, very highly dressed.'

Following consultation with historian Anne Choma, a specialist on Lister, Pye investigated period clothing at various museums, including Bath Museum, Chertsey Museum and Winchester City Museum. He also worked with Cosprop,

top right Distressed at being rejected by Walker, Lister flees England and travels to Copenhagen where, in an ostentatious black dress, she is presented to Queen Marie of Denmark (Sofie Gråbøl), who asks if she has always worn black. Lister replies that she has done so ever since she lost her first love. The queen commands her to stop mourning and tells her that she must wear white for the monarch's birthday ball. In stark and unexpected contrast to her daily attire, Lister celebrates her new-found freedom from grief by flirting with her dance companion, Sophie Ferrall (Stephanie Hyam), in a white gown that conforms to the style of the period, with a low *décolletage* and capped, puffed pleated sleeves.

below right Siblings of Lister's rivals, the disreputable Rawson brothers, Catherine (Emma Paetz, left) and Delia (Daisy-Edgar Jones) are enjoying afternoon tea. The leisured classes were deemed capable only of the most sedentary of pastimes, such as embroidery or watercolour painting. Dresses were invariably worn off the shoulder, with ruffles and frills added to bateau necklines to extend their width. The contrast of shoulder width to cinched waist is emphasized by voluminous sleeves, most commonly the gigot (leg-of-mutton) sleeve introduced in 1830. These were full from shoulder to elbow, the fullness supported by a small whalebone pannier tied to the shoulder, and fitted at the wrist.

the costume house of Oscar-winning costume designer and costumier John Bright.

Lister is first seen in action driving a high-flyer coach dangerously fast over the cobbles of the Yorkshire town of Shibden. The title of the TV series is the local nickname given to her. She is owner of Shibden Hall, which she inherits from her uncle, bypassing her inept father and younger sister, Marian (Gemma Whelan).

A chance meeting with timid and wealthy heiress, Ann Walker (Sophie Rundell), leaves Lister keen to form a lasting relationship with her, inviting gossip and social censure of their increasingly intimate relationship. Their connection flounders when Walker is persuaded by her friend, Harriet Parkhill (Elle McAlpine) that her feelings for Lister are wicked and that she should marry Thomas Ainsworth (Brendan Patricks), a curate and the widower of her best friend. He is a man who had previously made love to her while he was still married. Only following the encouragement

of Walker's married sister, Elizabeth Sutherland (Katherine Kelly), during a sojourn in Scotland, do the lovers, Walker and Lister, reconnect, illegally taking the marriage sacrament together in a small church in York. Afterwards, the couple continue to flout convention when Walker moves into Shibden Hall to live with Lister.

above Agnes (left) and Ada attend a ball, one of the many held during the height of the season. The ball dominated the social calendar of nineteenth-century New York, with attendance required two or three times a week. Evidencing the conspicuous consumption of the era and a desire to be irreproachable in her chosen garb, Ada wears mauve, a favourite colour of Queen Victoria since its invention by English chemist William Henry Perkin after he discovered the first commercial synthetic organic dye, mauveine, in 1856. The women wear opera gloves, which extend over the elbow and are fastened with a small row of rouleaux loops at the wrist. These could be undone to release the hands for using a knife and fork, the remainder of the gloves still in place.

THE GILDED AGE

KASIA WALICKA-MAIMONE (2022–)

The term 'Gilded Age' is used to describe the period after the American Civil War (1861–1865) when there was an economic boom and wealth was amassed through railroads, steamboats and oil, hence the title of Julian Fellowes' creation. The drama chronicles the competition for social eminence between the 'shoddy millionaires' with new money such as the Rockefellers and the Vanderbilts and the old, established families of 1880s New York society led by Caroline Schermerhorn Astor (Donna Murphy).

Costume designer Kasia Walicka-Maimone and her team of sixty-five assistants researched the periods before and after the golden age to produce approximately 5,000 costumes for the show's first season. This was a demanding task in view of the extraordinarily lavish embellishment and complicated cutting involved in constructing the garments. In the mid-1880s, there was a revival of the bustle protruding from the small of the back; the waist was ferociously tight-laced and emphasised with a horizontal drape of fabric at the front. The designer describes how the values of the two factions are expressed through what they wore:

'The distinction between the "old money" and "new money" characters can be seen through types of fabrics, colours and ornamentation in the costumes.'

The new money is epitomised by Bertha Russell (Carrie Coon), wife of the railway tycoon and robber baron George (Morgan Spector). She exemplifies the brash new world

top left Always desirous of being centre stage and eager to dominate the social scene in vividly colourful sculptural gowns that often display a diagonal feature epitomising the sharpness of her interactions with those around her is the calculating, ambitious and encroaching Bertha. She wears a dramatic, sensuous, serpentine gown in chartreuse, halfway between green and yellow and first described as a colour in 1884. As a young girl, Gladys Russell (Taissa Farmiga, left) is allowed to let down her back hair and wears age-appropriate white.

centre left Flanked by Caroline 'Carrie' Astor (Amy Forsyth) and his cousin Larry Russell (Harry Richardson, right), Oscar (Blake Ritson) deviates from the striped blazers and boaters worn by young men for their games of croquet on the lawns at Newport – the chosen summer resort of the oldest and most distinguished of the families – and expresses his eccentricity in a sharply cut maroon blazer, cream-linen waistcoat and trousers and a straw trilby.

below left Exemplifying the designer's intention that historical costume in film is made to be looked at and not worn, Bertha poses in a day dress in ice-blue silk satin. The bodice features a stomacher, which is a triangular panel set in the opening of a bodice that was a style prevalent in the eighteenth century. The gown displays all the excessive use of *passimentarie* made popular by influential couturier Worth: his close association with the French textile-and-trimming producers of Lyons resulted in a prolific use of luxurious materials and excessive decoration.

opposite Gladys and her older brother Larry (Harry Richardson) welcome Marian – who has crept out of the house unbeknown to her aunts – to Bertha's at-home, an invitation spurned by the members of the oldest families. Their dresses are simpler in detail and silhouette than those worn by their more mature counterparts. The young Gladys has yet to come out in society, so is in *ingénue* lilac. The extra fabric of the skirt of her dress is pulled to the small of her back to create a bustle, kept in place with a braided wire. As a poor relation, Marian, in pale, buttercup yellow, owns no family jewellery and instead ties a matching ribbon around her neck, wearing it as a choker.

with a brazen flaunting of wealth, expressed through vibrant colours and bold statements, desperately trying to impress the old-money world with excessive adornment.

The fashionable of the newly affluent elite of North America were clients of British-born Parisian couturier Charles Frederick Worth, who also dictated the fashions of the *haut monde* of Europe. Some willingly undertook the sea voyage to Paris for the time-consuming fittings, others had the garments fitted in New York. Old money waits until the fashions are less startlingly new.

Introduced into this milieu is Marian Brook (Louisa Jacobson). Orphaned and left penniless by the death of her father, she leaves her home in Pennsylvania and moves to New York to live with her two aunts, the acerbic Agnes van Rhijn (Christine Baranski) and the gentler Ada Brook (Cynthia Nixon). On her journey, Marian becomes friends with an African American young woman and ambitious writer, Peggy Scott (Denée Benton), who takes on the role of social secretary to Agnes. In contrast to the old-money décor – Louis XIV

furniture and Sèvres porcelain – of the aunts' house on 61st Street, the newly built house on Fifth Avenue, over the road, owned by the Russell family, is a vast marbled edifice perceived as ostentatious and vulgar. Bertha triumphs, however, and the old-money families, including Mrs Astor, eventually succumb to the lure of Bertha's invitations.

DOWNTON ABBEY

SUSANNAH BUXTON, ROSALIND EBBUTT,
CAROLINE MCCALL, ANNA ROBBINS (2010–2015)

above The clothes of the imperious and acerbic Dowager Countess of Grantham, the matriarch of the family, hark back to earlier days. She wears the flat-fronted corset fashionable at the turn of the century, beginning just below the bust – the effect is of a monobosom. The high-necked, white, frilled-lace and ribbon blouse adheres to the Edwardian precept of covering the body from head to toe during the day. The countess is also adorned with a vertical turban, or toque, of decorated lilac net, made fashionable by Queen Mary in 1910.

opposite Evidencing the more relaxed silhouette after the constraints of the S-shaped corset, the Crawley sisters adopt the newly fashionable longer, looser line emphasized with pleating, wrapping and gentle folds, giving greater freedom of movement. They wear non-boned 'afternoon' or 'tea apparel' dresses in pastel colours and diaphanous materials. Mary (centre), being the eldest, is allowed a deeper neckline, in contrast to her younger sister Edith (left), demure in a squared-off neckline and puffed sleeves. The avant-garde Sybil (right) is the most fashionable of the sisters, the more modern silhouette of her dress – a wrap bodice and rounded shoulder line in a small-scale print – having a high waist marked with a feature belt.

C reated and co-written by Julian Fellowes, the global TV phenomenon *Downton Abbey* is a fantasy version of an interwar Britain in which both aristocrats and servants are complicit about their place in the social hierarchy of the time. The series is introduced with long tracking shots of the glorious interiors of Highclere Castle in Hampshire, the location for Downton Abbey, following the army of servants as they clean the rooms, make the fires, prepare breakfast and iron the morning papers.

Developments in fashion and style over the six seasons are realised by costume designers Susannah Buxton for the first season, for which she recreates the costumes of a post-Edwardian era, and Rosalind Ebbutt for seasons two and three. Moving the narrative on to post-World War I in seasons three and four, Caroline McCall describes the early 1920s and the shift in silhouette (continued by Anna Robbins in seasons five and six):

'I started researching the 1920s when I first joined Downton and that gave me my grounding in the decade in terms of its authenticity, not just the cut of a man's suit, for example, but the different variations of style. Once I was familiar with the characters, I developed their styles through homing in on specific fashion designers from the time....'

Seminal fashion moments are captured throughout the decades, from the adoption of Parisian couturier Paul

top left The owners of Downton Abbey Lord and Lady Grantham are dressed in white linens for a summer garden fete. A former 'dollar princess' – wealthy US heiresses were much sought after by the impoverished British aristocracy – Cora Crawley, Countess of Grantham (Elizabeth McGovern) wears a 'Merry Widow' hat. The original was made in 1907 for the actress Lily Elsie for the London premiere of the operetta *The Merry Widow* (*Die lustige Witwe*, 1905) by the influential London dressmaker Lucy, Lady Duff-Gordon, who practised under the name Lucile. She traded in Paris, London, Chicago and New York and became a favourite of royalty and the nobility, though with a preference for US clients. She is also credited with inventing the catwalk show with her fashion parades.

centre left For a visit to Downton following his enlisting at the onset of World War I in 1914, Matthew, heir to the estate, wears the so-called 'No. 10 Dress (Temperate mess dress)'. An alternative to the full dress uniform, it comprises a scarlet mess jacket with a black shawl collar and lapels with black accents on the cuff. It is worn with a deeply cut waistcoat and stiff-fronted shirt, a detachable collar and black tie. Mary wears a fitted but uncorseted lace dress in black, the over-the-elbow length sleeves featuring pale-lavender chiffon pulled through the ribbon ties.

below left When Cora's mother, the wealthy widow Martha Levinson (Shirley MacLaine), visits Downton, the Dowager Duchess attempts to assert her dominance over her. She is adorned with a diamond-set tiara, known in aristocratic circles as the 'family fender'. The tiara was an emblem of inherited wealth, an important symbol of power and only worn by married women. Martha is the source of Cora's generous dowry that secured Downton's future. More modern than the dowager, her hair is bobbed in the latest style, and her jewellery is an indication of her wealth.

Poiret's oriental pyjamas by Lady Sybil Crawley (Jessica Brown Findlay) to Lady Mary Crawley (Michelle Dockery) cropping her hair into a face-framing Eton crop. The upstairs of Downton is ruled by Robert Crawley, Earl of Grantham (Hugh Bonneville), overseen by the formidable Dowager Countess, Violet (Maggie Smith). The head of the household downstairs is the lugubrious butler, Charles Carson (Jim Carter). The drama unfolds with the sinking of the RMS *Titanic* in 1912, resulting in both the heir to Downton Abbey and his son being lost at sea. Their place is taken by the solidly middle-class solicitor Matthew Crawley (Dan Stevens), much to the resentment of the Granthams' eldest daughter Mary and her sisters Sybil and Edith (Laura Carmichael). Country house set pieces abound in the series. The advent of train travel meant the country house became more accessible, and the era heralded the heyday of lavish weekend house parties, shooting weekends, formal dinners entertaining foreign dignitaries and pursuits such as shooting and hunting, all of which required specific types of apparel from country tweeds to lavish ball gowns.

above The increasing physical activity of women demanded more practical clothing, an ethos embraced by Lady Mary as she becomes involved in running the estate. She wears a long-line jacket, in a windowpane check, with a matching ankle-length skirt. British tailors Redfern & Sons applied the principles of masculine dress to tailoring for women. Matching jackets and skirts were known as 'tailor-mades', and cut from sturdy fabrics such as plaid, herringbone tweed or serge, and linen in summer. Matthew sports a front-pleated Norfolk jacket primarily worn for the outdoor pursuits enjoyed by the aristocracy, a design innovation made popular by King Edward VII.

above Linda dresses up for the coming-out ball of her eldest sister Louise (Beattie Edmondson). Disappointed and bored at the dreariness of the event – the other guests consist of her father's elderly cronies from the House of Lords – she is wearing a homemade version of the-then fashionable *robe de style*, the signature style of the French couturier Jeanne Lanvin. The designer revived the panniered, drop-waisted silhouette of the eighteenth century in the 1920s.

opposite above Bored with motherhood, Linda flings herself into a whirl of social gaiety 'frittering away the years of her youth' encouraged by her lifelong friend, neighbour and mentor Lord Merlin (Andrew Scott), an artist, musician, patron and one of the Bright Young Things of the era. Now known as a society beauty and flattered by the attentions of a series of young men, Linda parties in a bias-cut slither of cream silk satin and a silk kimono with a floral-placement print.

THE PURSUIT OF LOVE

SINÉAD KIDAO (2021)

Based on the semi-autobiographical novel of the same name written by English socialite Nancy Mitford in 1945, the series first introduces us to the two female protagonists, Linda Radlett (Lily James) and Fanny Logan (Emily Beecham) as they step over the rubble of a war-torn London in 1941, both pregnant. Set mainly at a time of uncertainty between the two World Wars, *The Pursuit of Love* is written, directed and executive produced by British actor Emily Mortimer.

Costume designer Sinéad Kidao acknowledges the diverse lives of the friends by their wardrobe choices.

'Linda and her siblings are wild and bored... what they wear is a bit erratic and messy, a mix of hand-me-down tweeds, jodhpurs and riding boots... As they grow up and go in different directions, Linda's style regularly changes. We felt that Linda was always "dressing the part", particularly in her adult years, from the glamorous socialite in the early 1930s, to life as a communist and then as a mistress in Paris.'

Linda vacillates between unkempt childhood jodhpurs and sweaters and dour grey suits when she flirts with being a communist, finally appearing as a fashionable mistress to a wealthy man. Fanny, married to an Oxford don, perfectly represents an upper-middle-class gentlewoman of the era in neat well-cut tweeds in autumnal colours, belted knitted

above Fanny visits Linda at her 'pretty little doll's house' on Cheyne Walk, a gift from Lord Merlin. The two friends sit on a bottle-strewn rooftop in the midst of a party for her communist friends. Fanny has made an effort to dress up for the occasion in a purple velvet opera cloak and beaded dress, but Linda is clothed in her well-worn, check wool coat with a red fox-fur collar and her beret, a mark of her left-wing affiliations.

cardigans and flat, sensible shoes. Her husband remarks that she is like the royal family: 'Whatever you wear you look exactly the same.'

The story is shown in flashback and is based on Mitford's eccentric family. The Radlett family is ruled by Linda's father and Fanny's detested uncle, the paterfamilias, Matthew, Lord Alconleigh (Dominic West). He is determined that no daughter of his should have any kind of life beyond the house and he has no truck with education for girls. The children find consolation from his rages in the linen cupboard, the only warm room in the house, where they meet together as 'Hons', so-called because as children of a peer they are entitled to the use of 'The Honourable' before their name.

In a desperate attempt to escape, Linda hurtles from one relationship to another, finally finding love with Fabrice, Duke de Sauveterre (Assaad Bouab). Once Linda becomes his mistress, she is festooned with a plethora of furs and Bulgari jewels – one necklace contains more than 500 diamonds and 112 akoya pearls – and silk-satin bias-cut evening dresses, a silhouette then made fashionable by Parisian couturier Madeleine Vionnet. However, her happiness lasts for only a few short months before he is killed in World War II, leaving her pregnant with his child, and she returns to Alconleigh where she lives with Fanny, but later dies in childbirth.

THE CROWN

MICHELE CLAPTON, JANE PETRIE,
AMY ROBERTS (2016–)

above Suffused with a golden light when re-enacted for
The Crown, the coronation of Queen Elizabeth II (Claire
Foy) was transmitted to 27 million TV viewers in black and
white. Court dressmaker Norman Hartnell, who designed
her wedding dress in 1947, was asked to produce a garment along the same lines in white satin. The fabric was
embellished with eleven symbolic motifs, among them
the English Tudor rose, the Scottish thistle, the Welsh
leek and the Irish shamrock. All were embroidered in silk,
incorporating seed pearls, diamonds, crystal, silver- and
gold-bullion thread and opals. According to Hartnell's
autobiography, the queen's comment on seeing the gown
for the first time was 'Glorious'. *The Crown* producers hired
a replica dress from Angels Costumes that was commissioned by Swarovski for the Queen's Diamond Jubilee in
2012 and displayed at Harrods. The dress was digitally
printed then enhanced with surface embroidery.

opposite Designed in the utmost secrecy by husband-
and-wife team David and Elizabeth Emanuel, Lady Diana
Spencer's wedding gown in Sudbury-woven, silk taffeta
featured a 25-foot train, the longest in the history of
royal wedding dresses and an indication of her dream to
be perceived as a fairy-tale princess. It was embellished with 10,000 mother of pearl sequins and pearls.
A 153-yard tulle veil was attached to the Spencer family
tiara, assembled in 1930 by Garrard from several old
Spencer diamond jewels. The iconic dress provided the
template for 1980s brides but later came to be derided
as a 'meringue'.

Peter Morgan's mega-budget blockbuster, *The Crown*,
is an exploration of Queen Elizabeth II and her seven
decades on the throne as the longest-reigning monarch, played variously by Claire Foy, Olivia Colman and
Imelda Staunton. Factual historical events provide the
backdrop to what is essentially a high-quality soap opera of
a family living a life of unimaginable luxury while also being
perpetually in crisis. Personal calamities are juxtaposed
with affairs of the crown, state and church. The historical
drama opens with the illness and death of King George VI
(Jared Harris) in 1952 and the coronation of his eldest
daughter Elizabeth the following year.

When designing for a biopic of the most photographed
family in history, there is a wealth of documented evidence
to guide the designers to recreate, stitch for stitch, the lines
of the original garment or outfit, while being given creative
leeway in certain private scenes where coherent speculation is necessary. Michele Clapton (ten episodes) and Jane
Petrie (ten episodes) were succeeded as costume designer
by Amy Roberts (thirty episodes), who points out:

> *'You can go from forensic accuracy, like with
> the queen's military uniform, to flights of fancy
> and glamour – it's an extraordinary programme
> for doing that.'*

The queen's personal trajectory from *ingénue* princess to
elderly monarch is reflected in the changing hues of her

above left The abdication of King Edward VIII (Alex Jennings) led to the crowning of his brother George as king. Edward was created Duke of Windsor and he married twice-divorced Wallis Simpson (Lia Williams) for whom he had renounced the throne. The couple led a life of exile in Europe and the Bahamas. Their vacuous existence of disappointment and ennui, was leavened only by their interest in sophisticated dress and an overblown lifestyle. A self-obsessed rebel in loud checks, the duke railed against the constrictions of dress that reflected his family's world of rigid convention. All his tailored clothing came from Dutchman Frederick Scholte, whose house style was defined by a softly tailored drape cut and rounded, natural sleeve head. Always impeccably groomed, his wife was famed for her love of couture, and was a client of Mainbocher and Schiaparelli.

above right Princess Margaret (Vanessa Kirby) waits nervously for Antony Armstrong-Jones, who is about to take her photograph. She wears a seductive bronze sheath dress with a deep cowl neckline gathered into the shoulder seams. In a scene taut with sexual tensions, the photographer peels back the shoulder bands so that the princess seems naked in the subsequent shot, causing outrage in the royal family when the photograph appears in the national press.

wardrobe. These evolve from pastels in the early 1960s to the mature, sober colours appropriate to her age that further reflect periods of social gloom in the 1970s and 1980s. As the series progresses, the queen is portrayed as a more formidable, obdurate figure, expressed by a hairstyle that segues from soft, feminine waves to a helmet-like construction from which it never deviated until her death.

Privately, the queen deals with the early frustration with his role felt by Prince Philip, Duke of Edinburgh (Matt Smith, Tobias Menzies, Jonathan Pryce). She also has to contend with the marital disharmony of Princess Margaret (Vanessa Kirby, Helena Bonham Carter, Lesley Manville) and the divorces of three of her four children.

High fashion is introduced into the series with the emergence of Princess Margaret, an early adopter of Christian Dior's New Look. Imbued with the poignant tragedy of her thwarted relationship with Group Captain Peter Townsend (Ben Miles), a divorcee, the princess was a romantic figure and renowned for her glamorous lifestyle. Her marriage to the fashionable photographer Antony Armstrong-Jones (Matthew Goode, Ben Daniels) in the 1960s further reinforced her fashion credentials. Princess

136   HISTORICAL

Anne (Erin Doherty) made an unlikely style icon as she was depicted in the third and fourth series of *The Crown*. Turning eighteen in 1968, the princess elevated her hemlines and adopted crisp, contemporary tailoring for her royal duties. The rediscovery of Princess Anne's track record as a transient arbiter of style reached a neat conclusion in 2022 when Buckingham Palace took the opportunity to post a gallery of her style highlights on the royal family's official Instagram account.

Towards the end of the fourth season, the unofficial separation of Charles, Prince of Wales (Josh O'Connor) and Diana, Princess of Wales (Emma Corrin) marks Diana's personal evolution from a naive teenage nanny in yellow dungarees to mature sophisticate and global icon in a tuxedo-style black dress or in the contour couture of Versace. These costumes form an eloquent contribution to the depiction of her transition to independent fame.

above left A state visit by the youthful President Kennedy (Michael C. Hall) and the First Lady (Jodie Balfour) emphasises the difference in style between the queen in her over-fussy evening gown with frilled chiffon bodice, designed by Hartnell, and the modern streamlined aesthetic preferred by Jacqueline Kennedy. She appears in a columnar dress of ice-blue satin, the original garment designed by New York-based Chez Ninon. The replica was designed to be strapless rather than featuring the boat neckline of the original. Unlike the queen, the fashion icon wore little jewellery, thinking it *démodé* and ageing. The costumes make a subtle social reflection on the bright New World putting the Old World in the shade.

above right Evolving from 'Shy Di' to media darling on the tour of Australia in 1983, while reputedly infuriating her husband Charles with her popularity, the Princess of Wales begins to understand her power in terms of her fashion choices and related exposure. Wearing a waterfall-frilled gown by her favourite British designer, Bruce Oldfield, she is twirled around the dance floor. Costume designer Roberts found it challenging to replicate the weight and colour of the fabrics worn on the tour, which were difficult to source.

above Heading out for a picnic, Hortense's friend Celia Langley (Nikki Amuka-Bird, left) wears a pink, polka-dot dress featuring a crossover bodice attached to a wide curved band at the midriff. The shoulder pads in the fitted sleeves add an element of elegance and glamour to her considered appearance, as do the pink and white matching beads. Hortense appears much less sophisti-cated and worldly as she promenades in white-crochet confirmation gloves, wearing an easy-fitting printed cotton dress with a Peter Pan collar, buttoned up to the neck, with her hair falling loose beneath her floral straw hat. Gilbert is relaxed in the manner of his dress; freed of his tie, he confirms his independent spirit with a sharp newsboy cap and toning cream linen jacket and brown trousers.

above On a brief visit to Queenie, Michael strides out in a demob version of the zoot suit made popular by urban African Americans in the 1940s – the word 'zoot' being a reduplication of the word 'suit'. Zoot-suit features include a single-breasted jacket with exaggerated lapels, body panels cut in a long-line, tapering at the waist, and full trousers tamed into a cuff at the ankle. His wide-brimmed hat is tipped back on the head while the brim is flipped down racily at the front. This jaunty manner is mirrored by the angle of Queenie's chenille beret and by her outfit of flounced dress under a square shouldered gaberdine jacket, box-pleated in the back and fitted to the waist.

SMALL ISLAND

LORNA MARIE MUGAN (2009)

A drab and gloomy, bomb-ravaged London provides a stark counterpoint to the cerulean blue skies and vibrant colours of the Caribbean in British author Andrea Levy's *Small Island,* adapted from her novel of the same title of 2004. Irish designer Lorna Marie Mugan, exploits the bright cheeriness, under the Jamaican sun, of cotton-print dresses, straw hats and the leisured airiness of men's linen jackets to strike a contrast to the dour realities of post-war London in the era of 'make do and mend'. She outlines her basic ethos as the costume designer on a project:

> *'There is a big responsibility to honour the director's vision for the script; integrate seamlessly with production design and camera; deliver quality on a limited budget and forge a relationship of trust with the cast. If they don't believe that the costumes belong to the character, no one else will.'*

Post-war London is an environment of dismal streets indented with bomb sites and a domestic culture of clothes rationing and standardisation, under the aegis of the Ministry of Supply's Utility Mark for manufactured goods, which included garments. Jamaican society and fashion in the 1940s was largely in thrall to external influences – not least an unreciprocated attachment to the British mother country in the fading sunset of its empire. Recollections of colonial loyalty afforded to the British monarchy and

top left Under a well-worn, fisherman's-rib cardigan, Queenie's shell-shocked father-in-law, Arthur (Karl Johnson), wears a Fair Isle sleeveless sweater. This was a home-grown wardrobe staple in wartime, when clothing rationing was in place and odds and ends of wool could be used for the complex, multicoloured pattern of the knit. Queenie sports a Veronica Lake hairdo – named after the wartime US film star. She matches the pink of her polka-dot blouse with two-tone buttons and pink Cornely work – a type of freehand machine embroidery – on the reveres of her waistcoat.

below left Meeting her new landlady, Queenie, in the dimly lit surroundings of her rundown house, Hortense becomes downcast having arrived from Jamaica. Intent on projecting courtesy and self-respect, Hortense has dressed up for the journey in a turquoise wool, crêpe skirt-suit cut along the military lines of the 1940s, accessorised with a stylish hat. Queenie signals the untold drudgery of her existence: she is revealed wearing a faded print housedress – an overgarment worn to protect the clothes beneath during household chores. It has lost its original waisted shape as the shirred elastic of the smocking surrenders to age and the once-interesting distribution pattern of buttons has lost its rhythm. Her high-neck sweater is in a classic DIY hand-knit stitch of feather and fan lace.

opposite Dressed in deferential formality for her interview with the Board of Education, Hortense is ambitious to advance her career and life aspirations. She is perfectly groomed in a demure belted coat in eau-de-Nil wool crêpe, worn over a peach damask dress. Her accessories are considered with equal care, she teams white gloves – no longer in juvenile crochet – and a classic pearl-white handbag with a precisely positioned brooch and a natural straw hat. Her bubble of optimism is burst when they determine that her Jamaican teaching qualifications are not valid in Britain. Gilbert is also presented as the epitome of English suburban respectability – a measured elegance in understated tailoring. His grey–blue, RAF-toned three-piece suit is in a textured worsted hopsack cloth worn over a quiet, hickory-stripe shirt and *ton-sur-ton* patterned tie. He wears a level-headed trilby hat in rose taupe that chimes with the windowpane shadow check of his fastidiously constructed overcoat. This has a softer silhouette created by the raglan sleeve-head and top stitched cuffs that draw the eye to his military-style wristwatch.

affectations of idealised English manners provided rich sources of costume inspiration. Wallis, Duchess of Windsor, the noted celebrity clotheshorse, while sequestered in the Bahamas with her husband, lent an elevated air of gentility to garden parties by adding the mannered accessories of sun hat, pearls, short, white gloves, and court shoes. This ensemble was perceived as a template for the proper manner of dress – more English than the English, even if home-sewn – for any public event in Jamaica. For men, the duke provided a model for the adoption of light, natural linen suits. A less-elevated menswear stimulation was the presence of US sailors and airmen, at leisure in Kingston from their new bases on the island.

The story moves to and fro between Jamaica and England. Gilbert Joseph (David Oyelowo) and Michael Roberts (Ashley Walters), young Jamaican men with a fierce loyalty to England, sign up to fight alongside the British in World War II. Queenie Bligh (Ruth Wilson) is married to Bernard (Benedict Cumberbatch), a well-heeled bank manager living with his shell-shocked father. When the war intervenes, Bernard enlists in the Royal Air Force (RAF) and

Queenie has three airmen billeted with her, one of whom is Michael. The two become passionately involved before he is deployed on his next mission.

Gilbert returns to Jamaica at the end of the war, only to be tempted by the British government's offer of a cheap passage to England, which was a strategy to fill post-war labour shortages. He travels on the HMT *Empire Windrush*, arriving on 21 June 1948 at Port of Tilbury, Essex, with 1,027 other passengers, 539 of whom are from Jamaica. Hortense (Naomie Harris), the illegitimate daughter of an affluent white governor and his servant of colour, follows Gilbert; they both move in with Queenie.

After the war, Michael returns to spend a weekend with Queenie before emigrating to Canada and leaving her pregnant. Following the shocking reappearance of Bernard, who Queenie assumes was killed in the war, she goes into labour and has a dark-skinned baby, whom she names 'Michael'. As Queenie reluctantly hands him over to Gilbert and Hortense to bring up as their own, she slips a photograph of herself into the carry cot, which is later seen in the photograph album belonging to her son.

above Actor Tabu, as she is known, plays the Muslim singer of note and long-established courtesan, Saeeda Bai. She entertains the attentions of young, impetuous and devoted Maan, who is Hindu and of the bourgeois Kshatriya caste. At ease in the privacy of her boudoir, they are each dressed in unusual richness, suggestive of languor and indulgence. Their mutual colour palette recalls both Mughal paintings and those of US abstract of US abstract artist Mark Rothko, which the costume designer acknowledges as inspirations. Saeeda is draped in a silk *kantha* stitch *dupatta* (stole) over a *kameez* (tunic) in citrus damask silk and *dhoti shalwar* (wrapped pants) in emerald damask. Maan wears a long peacock damask *kurta* over slender white muslin *churidar* (trousers) and under a dark patterned *bundi* (gilet).

above Within the codified framework of Sanskrit performing arts there are eight categories of *nayika* (heroine), including Vipralabdha – a heroine deceived or disappointed by the non-appearance of her lover. In this outfit which adheres to the conventional depiction of a Vipralabdha, Saeeda conveys an air of introspection and disillusion, setting aside her jewellery and adopting the simplicity of a white muslin *kameez*, swathed under a figured red muslin *dupatta*, also in cotton muslin. Unlike most of the other female characters in the drama, Saeeda predominantly allows her hair to hang free, reflecting the common depiction of courtesans in Mughal paintings.

A SUITABLE BOY
ARJUN BHASIN (2020)

The screen adaptation of Vikram Seth's 1,500-page epic Indian novel *A Suitable Boy* (1993) demanded exceptional powers of synopsis from screenwriter, Andrew Davies. Likewise, the costume designer, Arjun Bhasin, was charged with codifying the complexity of the hierarchical, social and political nuances of mid-century Indian costume to depict the positioning of 105 speaking parts and a myriad of extras across the social spectrum. He was fortunate that contemporary retail sources could provide traditional apparel, such as classic hand-loomed saris. Wardrobe also has to reveal much of the context of the broad scope of the chronicle, which famously has an exclusively non-white cast. Bhasin explains his process:

> *'We did crazy amounts of research. I always start with the script, the page, and then load up on research. Some of the research translates directly into costumes, and some of it just situates you in the period. You familiarise yourself with the rules. Then you start playing with the rules, start creating characters and character arcs.'*

The drama is set in the tumult of India from 1951 to 1952, newly post-independence and post-partition. In a sense, it is a coming-of-age narrative both of a nation and of the nineteen-year-old student and protagonist, Lata Mehra (Tanya Maniktala), who, at the core of the saga, attempts to resist her mother's desire to choose a spouse

top left Undergraduates at large in Brahmpur, Lata and close friend Malati (Sharvari Deshpande), clutch their academic intentions to heart by accessorising their student garb with novel and notebook respectively, at a glance identifying their English Literature or Medical Science credentials. Lata wears a richly embroidered, crimson *kurta* tunic over loose *dhoti* wrapped pants, trailing behind a lengthy *dupatta* stole with banded patterning at either hem. Her worldly and adventurous friend, Malati, wears a cotton *jamdani* sari with sparse patterning in aqua cotton muslin over a clinical white *choli* (blouse).

centre left Haresh Khanna (Namit Das) is proposed as a suitor to Lata, with the approval of her mother Rupa (Mahira Kakkar). Lata indulges her mother's wishes to the extent of agreeing to visit the shoe manufacturing company that Haresh manages. Rupa is swathed in textured ecru cotton – the colour of widows' saris – and Lata echoes her mother's choice with the addition of a check *choli* and a pop of colour – signifying youthful status. Haresh reveals his basic anglophile wardrobe: a faint, gauche influence from the Duke of Windsor underlies his crumpled double-breasted sport coat worn with knitted waistcoat.

below left The wedding party is over and it is time for the Mehra brothers to remove their pink party turbans. Meenakshi Chatterji-Mehra is to be guided quickly back to Calcutta by charmless husband Arun (Vivek Gomber). Now upwardly mobile, Arun is at pains to hold to Western dress in a sharply tailored single-breasted jacket, bulbous double-Windsor-knotted tie and taut, fully buttoned waistcoat as he finds himself in the milieu of international finance and business suits. Varun wears a red wedding *kurta* coat over *churid*ar fitted trousers in white. Meenakshi is fully at ease in her self-esteem and status as a modern married Brahmin. The rich dark hues of her hand-loomed sari – draped *nivi*-style with the end thrown back over her left shoulder – and the low-cut *choli* in crimson confirm, together with her bindi dot on her forehead, that she is a married woman of substance.

opposite Lata is swept off her feet by her brother-in-law, Amit Chatterji (Mikhail Sen), a Cambridge-trained lawyer *manqué*, turned languid poet/author. Amit has a tailored wardrobe that is expensively well-cut, which he wears with an air of entitlement and dissipation. Lata adopts the *nivi* style of sari draping favoured by her sophisti-cated upscale relative, Meenakshi. In this instance, her sari is diaphanous with embroidered rosettes, worn in sufficient profusion – where gathered – to become opaque. But it remains flirtatiously transparent when the final single thickness length is thrown from the hip over the left shoulder to reveal a naked midriff below the sleeveless, cropped *choli* blouse.

for her. The vast range of the story – from intimate or familial undercurrents to macro-scale religious, legal and cultural dynamics of Indian life – demands that exposition is multilayered. The burden of depiction is leavened by the sophisticated signage in clothing and textiles sourced by Bhasin. Costume is used to expose the fault lines between segment castes, generations and localised cultures. There was a large range of signifiers in Indian costume and textiles in the 1950s and every aspect speaks, from the ankle-revealing sari that tells of a commitment to labour and low status, to the use of red to express joy and for weddings. Even within the designed options of pattern distribution in the flat rectangle of a sari cloth, there are implicit signs of social status.

The opening scenes of the first episode concern the wedding of Lata's elder sister, Savita (Rasika Dugal), to Pran Kapoor (Gagandev Riar), who is the son of politician Mahesh (Ram Kapoor). It takes place in the elegant Mehra family home in the fictional provincial city of Brahmpur. The event is thronged with representatives from most of the plot lines and some of the caste groupings in the saga. The Brahmin caste is personified in Meenakshi Mehra, née Chatterji

(Shahana Goswami) visiting from Calcutta. She is the urbane, errant wife of Lata's arrogant elder brother, Varun (Vivaan Shah), who has married well and beyond their Kshatriya caste (warriors and administrators). The Nawab Sahib of Baitar (Aamir Bashir) – an important Muslim landowner – is present with his son, Firoz Ali Khan (Shubham Saraf), in turn the close friend of Maan Kapoor (Ishaan Khattar), a young Hindu Kshatriya, whose zest for life becomes pivotal in the drama. Many of the unspoken tensions in the plot are defined by clothing and by the significance of textile production in the fight for India's economic and political independence. Imperial Britain, through the East India Company, used tariffs to favour British yarn and fabric production in Manchester, in order to destroy the indigenous manufacture and compel India to import British cotton cloths. The leader of India's independence movement, Mahatma Gandhi, fought this injustice by encouraging the mass return to producing yarn and fabric by hand, promoting *khadi* cloth. The Swadeshi movement sought to boycott foreign goods to encourage the renaissance of Indian home-manufacture, and its ambition has since born fruit in the widest sense of global capitalism.

above Midge adheres to the precept that a façade of perfection has to be upheld at all times, with style diktats for every social and domestic function. Christian Dior's New Look was the first significant post-war fashion statement, the archetypal 1950s silhouette continued to be influential throughout the decade and beyond. Midge takes off her frilly organdie apron on her estranged husband's arrival to display the crisply engineered dress worn over stiffened petticoats.

opposite Midge's uncle runs a garment factory in the Seventh Avenue garment district, the source of many of her outfits. Her lively, wisecracking nature is represented by a wardrobe of saturated colour when things are going well, as with this loose-fitting, pink duster coat with dolman sleeves lined with blue, worn over a striped full-skirted dress. The duster coat was first seen at the turn of the twentieth century with the advent of the motor car, when it was worn to protect the clothes from the dirt and dust of road travel.

THE MARVELOUS MRS MAISEL

DONNA ZAKOWSKA (2017–)

Amy Sherman-Palladino's Emmy-winning comedy *The Marvelous Mrs Maisel* offers a dazzling vista of a vibrant post-war New York, with glittering skyscrapers, gleaming storefronts and bustling streets. The visual impact of the drama shares some of the breezy ebullience of the Doris Day movies *Pillow Talk* (1959) and *Lover Come Back* (1961) in the heightened pastel wardrobe of the eponymous heroine, Miriam 'Midge' Maisel (Rachel Brosnahan).

Emmy Award-winning New York-born costume designer Donna Zakowska describes Midge's trajectory from perfect Upper West Side housewife and mother of two to a groundbreaking, professional stand-up comedian.

'I spent a lot of time agonising over which colour she would be [wearing] in the next sequence... I used to make lots of little charts and actually put little colour swatches on it, and I'd watch the pattern of the colours and when they appeared. I'd sort of be tracking her emotional strength or assertiveness or lack of in the colours.'

Midge is contentedly married to Joel (Michael Zegen), trained by her mother to uphold standards of both domesticity and appearance; her look is achieved by waking up before her husband to apply full make-up and unpin her hair. He is an aspiring stand-up comedian. Once she discovers that he is having an affair with his secretary, she ceases

top left Midge's mother, Rose Weissman (Marin Hinkle), takes afternoon tea at the garden club with friends, surrounded by an exquisite array of floral hats. There, she discovers her matchmaking skills and develops them into a burgeoning new enterprise. Always committed to aesthetic perfection, she wears a belted jacket with a deep tailored collar and matching accessories.

centre left In the foyer of the chic Fontainebleau Hotel, Miami Beach, Susie remains loyal to her Gaslight Café aesthetic in a leather jacket and newsboy cap. The keys to the Gaslight club that hang around her neck are her only jewellery. Midge continues to uphold her sartorial standards and impeccable grooming with a vibrant print sheath dress with floating chiffon panels attached to the shoulders.

below left Midge and her mother Rose assess what they will need for a two-month sojourn in the Catskill Mountains. The summer resorts there were a traditional vacation spot for New York Jewish families. Midge holds up a turquoise, polka-dot bikini, saying: 'Should I go classy… or *risqué*?' Influenced by US sex symbol Mamie Van Doren, she decides to go *risqué*, rather than opting for demure gingham. Although introduced in 1946, the bikini was still considered daring in the 1950s and was not generally accepted until the 1960s.

opposite Segueing into a looser, more modern silhouette, Midge wears cropped trousers and a pale, check coat with an oversize Peter Pan collar fastened with two large, fabric-covered buttons. Accosting a dapper gentleman at her side on the park bench, she asks him if he knows a bar 'where a lady can drink with another lady' before checking that he is not a policeman. He dismisses her fears, and gestures towards his cream linen suit, saying: 'This is Dior too.'

to facilitate his unsuccessful career and embarks on one of her own. Her first stop is to regale a Greenwich dive bar with a wisecracking monologue about her abandonment. She is taken into custody for her use of foul language and nudity, and at the police precinct she meets radical stand-up comedian and satirist Lenny Bruce (Luke Kirby), who becomes her mentor. When not wearing beatnik-inspired Capri pants and tight sweaters visiting the West Village, she develops a narrower, more svelte look of tailored dresses with the emphasis on the all-important matching accessories. Her decision not to alter her signature look when performing – usually in an Audrey Hepburn-inspired little black dress, over-the -elbow gloves and pearls that make her something of a novelty – confounds expectations. One impresario remarks: 'You just don't look funny.'

Midge's career is managed by Susie Myerson (Alex Borstein), an employee of the Gaslight Café where she first performs her act. Midge goes on tour, abruptly abandoning her fiancé Benjamin Ettenberg (Zachary Levi) and leaving her children with her ex-husband. She first entertains the troops on a military base and subsequently appears as the opening act for popular singer Shy Baldwin (LeRoy McClain) in Las Vegas and Miami Beach, where her wardrobe epitomises a West Coast glamour with Hepburn-style sunglasses and a black Lastex maillot. All set for stardom, Miriam – no longer Midge – mistakenly outs Shy to his adoring audience. She is fired from the fame-making tour, ending back where she started, working dives in New York.

A VERY BRITISH SCANDAL

IAN FULCHER (2021)

above Neglected by the 10th Duke of Argyll, the monumental Inveraray Castle and its extensive grounds are restored at the expense of the duchess. On 25 April 1953, the castle opens its doors to the public to the sound of the regimental pipe band of the Argyll and Sutherland Highlanders. Greeting them at the door of the castle, the Duke of Argyll wears a kilt in the Clan Campbell tartan; the duchess echoes the ancestral heritage in a bias-cut skirt of the same cloth. This is worn below a tailored jacket cut in the style of Christian Dior's Le Bar, which debuted in 1947, over which is draped a sable shrug. Long-regarded as a sign of status and luxury, fur is also a tacit signifier of libido and erotic power. Her signature three-strand pearl necklace is accompanied by a pearl bracelet.

opposite At home in Inveraray Castle and away from scrutiny, the duchess dresses in a relatively casual manner. Her high-cut, covert cloth slacks with tailored slash pockets, are cinched by a broad belt to emphasise a nipped waist securing the soft folds of a pale, oyster-pink, Duchesse-silk blouse. The sleeves are gathered at cuff and shoulder and the quality of fluidity is sustained by a pussycat bow at the neck. The style is an echo of the garment in the portrait behind her.

Written and created by Sarah Phelps, the ravishingly shot drama *A Very British Scandal* recounts the period of one of the most scandalous court cases in legal history: the divorce between Ian Campbell, 11th Duke of Argyll (Paul Bettany), and Margaret, Duchess of Argyll (Claire Foy). It was his third marriage and her second. The duchess was a famed former débutante and, by the time of their divorce in 1963, she was already camera fodder: 2,000 people gatecrashed her first wedding in 1933 and she was celebrated in a song by Cole Porter 'You're the Top' (1934). Born Ethel Margaret Whigham, she was the only daughter of a fabulously wealthy textile industrialist – her father headed the manufacture of viscose acetate, a form of artificial silk – had been voted third in a list of the ten best-dressed women in Britain, following Wallis, Duchess of Windsor, and Princess Marina, Duchess of Kent. She exuded an overwhelming confidence in her own sex appeal, which was emphasised by her costumes designed by Ian Fulcher:

> '*I always kept the silhouette very figure-hugging because it was about her being empowered in her sexuality.*'

He preferred not to replicate the outfits worn by the duchess, of which there is much visual evidence – in the main she was habitually dressed by British court dressmaker Norman Hartnell and South African-born British couturier

above left Attending the duke's birthday party for his daughter by a previous marriage, the duchess wears a silk-satin dress with a wrapover pleated neckline. The duchess is adorned in her customary triple row of pearls. Before the 1950s, pearl necklaces were graduated, in later decades strands were more often of a uniform size. These are worn throughout the drama in every scene, including in the infamous 'headless man' photograph showing the duchess performing fellatio on an uniden-tified man. The necklace was used in evidence as proof of her identity.

above right Forbidden to enter the grounds of Inveraray Castle, the duchess is brought to a halt by the police at the bridge on the estate's perimeter. Exiting the car with her poodle in tow, she is seen wearing a burnt-orange, knee-length duster coat in Venetian wool with dropped shoulder seams and bound buttonholes; it envelops a fitted purple suit which has a matching birdcage-veiled, pillbox hat. The duchess' tailored outfits are consis-tently sexualised by feminine touches, in this case a leopard-print scarf.

Victor Stiebel. The series required eighty-five costume changes for the duchess, all of which were made specially, including shoes, gloves and hats. The strict tailoring of the period is softened with feminine touches such as a draped fur falling loosely off her shoulders and stand-away collars that emphasise her neck adorned in pearls.

On Margaret's marriage to Ian in 1951, he soon reveals himself to be a violent, vicious drunk, his volatile tempera-ment exacerbated by prescribed Drinamyl tablets, commonly known as 'purple hearts'. She herself was not averse to deception. Following the restoration of Inveraray Castle, which had been expedited by her own and her father's money, she learns that, on the death of the duke, she would have to leave the castle to his heirs from his second mar-riage. She therefore forges letters from his ex-wife, Louise (Sophia Myles), claiming that he is not the father of her sons.

Spending most of her time in London, Margaret enjoys a high-octane social life, for which she wears a series of beaded form-fitting couture gowns. The parties are described by her caustic friend Maureen Guinness, Mar-chioness of Dufferin and Ava (Julia Davis) as 'all cocktails

and cocks'. The same friend abandons her following the notorious and bitter divorce proceedings. These created extensive publicity and fuelled outrageous rumours and press opprobrium, particularly when, in his divorce petition, the duke lodged a list of eighty-eight of her alleged lovers. The presiding judge, John Wheatley, Lord Wheatley (Jonathan Aris), in his summing up of 50,000 words concluded that the duchess was a 'completely promiscuous woman' who engaged in 'disgusting sexual activities'.

above left The Argyll divorce case finally comes to court in 1963, at the Court of Session in Edinburgh. Striding defiantly to court to encounter the duke, the duchess wears a closely fitting burgundy suit with a back-slit pencil skirt and a single-breasted jacket with bracelet-length sleeves, accessorised with a matching birdcage-veiled pillbox hat worn on the back of the head. Replacing the boxy, top-handle handbags of the era with a slouchy bag held under the arm adds to the duchess' bravado, the bold impact sustained with a voluptuous silver fox stole, suede stilettos and kid opera gloves.

above right Faultlessly accessorised with court shoes, cocktail gloves and clutch bag in putty hues to tone with her pearls, the duchess wears a pale-slate sheath dress with a split at the centre-back hem, flagged by the heel seams of her fully-fashioned stockings. The dress is shrouded within a short, shawl-collared swing-back coat in a raised wool mouflon cloth in a blush shade. The swingback coat or jacket flourished from the late 1940s to the 1950s, inspired by Balenciaga and Dior. The *coup de grâce* of the harmonies of the outfit lies in the half-veiled and feathered Juliet cap; the neutrality of the overall look gives power to the dark brunette of her hair.

RETRO

One of the aims of the costume designer is to invite the suspension of disbelief; the more credible the costumes, the more the viewer is convinced by an unfamiliar world, recalled from a previous epoch. Scrupulously researched authenticity was the prerequisite demanded by Matthew Weiner, originator of the series *Mad Men* (see p 160), set in Manhattan, New York. Lit with a graphic clarity as if filmed unadorned in real time, the drama was hailed for the fidelity of its costuming. The series transitions from the early 1960s to the start of the 1970s, recording the fashions of the day in painstaking detail. This successful evocation of the sharp-tailored riches of the era resulted in a commercial spin-off by costume designer Janie Bryant with Banana Republic/GAP in 2011.

The drama series *The Queen's Gambit* (see p 156), conversely, is permeated with a sensation of unreality. Although set at the same time and on the same continent as *Mad Men*, the whole is suffused with a vintage sepia glow that shows the clothes, although similar, in a different light.

Symbiotic partnerships between commercial fashion and the small screen are exemplified by the biopic *Halston* (see p 166) and the flurry of sartorial activity inspired by the drama as Netflix produced a capsule collection drawn from archival Halston designs.

By contrast, the drama *The Deuce* (see p 174) had little relevance to modern life in terms of influencing fashion. The series projects a veneer of truthfulness in its depiction of the porn industry through its costumes, leaving the potential for fashion-trade tie-ins constrained by the subject matter.

Cinema icon Joan Crawford (Jessica Lange) is faithfully served in the biopic *Feud: Betty and Joan* (see p 170), a recounting of the notorious antagonism between the actor and her rival Bette Davis (Susan Sarandon). Crawford's

above Roger Sterling (John Slattery, left) and Don Draper (Jon Hamm) of *Mad Men* are depicted with exacting 1960s accuracy, nuanced as distinct characters sharing the setting of a TWA Boeing 707 jet and sitting in genuine period seats. Roger has taken the late-1960s gentleman-about-town codes of a dapper Brit, weekending in sharp, double-breasted, wool barathea blazer, check slacks and Chelsea boots. Don, though younger, remains firmly in his business attire, still clad as an early 1960s Cary Grant in a dark suit with black Oxford shoes and regimental stripe tie. The TWA Poppy flight-attendant uniforms are faithful to the originals manufactured from 1968 to 1971 by Dalton Apparel of Cleveland, Ohio.

inimitable style, which was *démodé* even then, captures the dying days of the Hollywood star system in defiance of any concept of modernity, which Davis, by contrast, so effortlessly engaged with in her casual slacks and easy-fitting sweaters.

Set during the AIDS epidemic of the 1980s, *It's a Sin* (see p 180) defaults from any notion of fashionability in a deliberate attempt in the production to depict the low-key, the ordinary and the wearable. Recent enough to be recalled by many viewers – albeit, for some, with the prompting of family photo albums – dramas featuring retro fashions fall open to criticism if the designer gets it wrong. Ephemeral detail can attract inordinate scrutiny; a hairline crack in the looking glass through which the viewer enters a different reality can fracture the illusion. An instance of this vulnerability is observed in *The Serpent* (see p 178) when the murderer's girlfriend, Marie-Andrée Leclerc (Jenna Coleman), a keen adherent to fashion, fails to pluck her naturally thick eyebrows into the thin, arched form fashionable in the 1970s – a style she could not fail to note on the models in the fashion magazines she devoured.

THE QUEEN'S GAMBIT

GABRIELE BINDER (2020)

above On her triumphant departure from Moscow, Beth (Anya Taylor-Joy) celebrates her victory over Russian chess grandmaster, Vasily Borgov (Marcin Dorocinski), by appearing as an incarnation of the White Queen. Gone are the persistent chequered references of her earlier career, she now stands triumphant above the field, the tip of a black roll-neck collar is the only acknowledgement of her defeated opponent. She presents a regal, monolithic figure, formed in white on white: white trousers, white gloves with a large, matching Basque beret. Her sculpted white coat has concealed fastenings buried under embossed circular forms, and, in adherence to the geometric theme and symbolic status, it has a squared-off mandarin collar.

opposite When Beth is in Paris, the Russian team goad her for being too glamorous to be a serious chess player. On a shopping spree, she wears a grey-flannel pinafore dress over a skinny, black turtleneck in the style of British designer Mary Quant. The midi-length duffel coat in a lofty tweed is worn long for the era, and displays a large, pastel pink-and-white check outlined in dove grey. The grid geometry is sustained with vertical pockets and yoke, and it is fastened duffel-style with four, outsize rouleaux button loops.

Adapted from a little-known novel of 1983 of the same name by Walter Tevis, and created as a TV miniseries by Scott Frank and Allan Scott, *The Queen's Gambit* is named after an opening strategy in chess. It is a coming-of-age story that begins in the 1950s and follows the trajectory of Beth Harmon (Annabeth Kelly, Isla Johnston, Anya Taylor-Joy) from child prodigy to unrivalled star of international chess. Orphaned at the age of nine after a car crash, she is sent to the dour and sterile Methuen Home for Girls in Kentucky. Here, her loneliness is assuaged by her friendship with fellow orphan, Jolene (Moses Ingram), and by the janitor, Mr Shaibel (Bill Camp), who introduces her to chess. In keeping with the appalling practices of the era, she is medicated into a state of docility by the resident nurse in the orphanage. Under this narcotic influence, Beth comes to realise that she can use her will to project an hallucinatory chessboard onto her dormitory ceiling, fully visualising complex moves and counter-strategies. In consequence, she conceives – and constantly practises – the dangerous belief that she needs to be under the influence of either drink or hallucinogenic drugs in order to succeed.

German costume designer Gabriele Binder establishes a pervasive leitmotif from the black and white squares of the chessboard, transposing the chequered pattern onto interior surfaces and clothes. Wallpaper grids provide

top left Dressed in the dispiriting orphanage uniform of a drab, green–grey, Quaker-style pinafore dress, Beth (Isla Johnston) fades into the institutional background, victim of the home's determination to suppress in their charges any individuality or self-expression. Sent on an errand to the basement, she discovers the caretaker, Mr Shaibel, in his careworn shabbiness, playing a solitary game of chess. Initially reluctant, he agrees to teach her how to play. When he realises how gifted she is, he introduces her to the local high-school chess-club teacher.

centre left Alma is Beth's adoptive and alcoholic mother; the jaded, neglected housewife takes Beth for her first clothes-shopping experience, although the rotary dress rail and wire bins have the glamour only of the discount store. Alma has an air of enervating nihilism, reinforced by the granite drabness of her costume of matching cocktail dress and duster coat in grey serge. Alma's despondency and indolence is mirrored in the choice of dreary colour palette she inflicts on Beth, whose weighty Titian red, pageboy bob steals the tonal scene.

below left Now claiming full ownership of the house in Kentucky, after buying out her adoptive father, Beth abandons herself to a prolonged drug and alcohol bender. Her decadence is personified in her schoolgirl camisole, swathed in an opulent camel-hair cardigan. She only surfaces with a visit from Jolene, who is now a paralegal. They attend the funeral of Mr Shaibel, calling in at the orphanage where Beth is distraught to discover that the janitor has been following her career and has adorned the basement walls with press cuttings of her achievements.

opposite In Las Vegas for the US Open, Beth plays the current national chess champion, Benny. Beth is sedately colour co-ordinated to this backdrop, wearing a beige pleated A-line skirt and a neatly fitting jersey top, contoured by contrasting stripes of French navy and pastel pink. It is framed into a 'V' at the back, cleverly providing interest to those spectating from behind. In contrast, Benny expresses his wholehearted role as a counter-cultural maverick with his barely-there moustache and large fedora. He enters the combat of the chess match sporting his 1940s vintage police motorcycle trench coat.

background support to chequered clothes in a variety of permutations and situations. This intriguing thematic thread later culminates in the deployment of a window-pane-checked coat by André Courrèges, a futuristic, French couturier of the 1960s, although Binder points out:

> 'Most of what you see on Anya Taylor-Joy was made
> for her, and the '60s were appealing to us because it
> was the first time when youth had owned fashion....'

Squared-off style lines and contours, bold geometric silhouettes and graphic patterns were all part of an expression of mid-1960s freedom and modernism in fashion, adopted by Space Age couturiers such as Pierre Cardin and Paco Rabanne. For many years, the rivalries of the Space Race and World Chess Championship were both emblematic of the miasma of Cold War hostilities between the United States and the Soviet Union.

Beth initially has little awareness of fashion when she is adopted in her teens by an unhappily married local couple. When the husband abandons his alcoholic wife, Alma Wheatley (Marielle Heller), she and Beth form a tenuous

connection that is strengthened when they embark on a series of chess tournaments across the United States, with Beth achieving ever-increasing success. As Beth evolves as a chess player, so too does her desire to be more fashionable. Youthquake fashions were adopted much later in the United States than in Britain and Beth continues to wear fitted shirt dresses, pleated skirts and tops with demure Peter Pan collars and cap sleeves into the mid-1960s. Only later, after a visit to her friend Benny Watts (Thomas Brodie-Sangster) in New York where he is training her for the Paris Invitational, she meets Cleo (Millie Brady), a model whose metallic tights and sleeveless, bronze, knitted minidress inspire her to adopt a more contemporary body-skimming style. The interiors are suffused with a subtle glow that gives the series a sepia-tinted, vintage feel – a pastiche of the sombre political perils of the period rather than a re-enactment.

MAD MEN

JANIE BRYANT (2007–2015)

Opening with a suited body in free-fall from a sky-scraper, the credits encapsulate the precipitous nature of the golden age of advertising in Matthew Weiner's series *Mad Men*. Every shot is a celebration of late Mid-century Modern style and considered for its aesthetic impact and period authenticity. Weiner's overarching vision spans an era from 1960 to 1970, recalled with meticulous attention to the minutiae of set and costume design, aided by Emmy Award-winning costume designer, Janie Bryant.

At the helm of a team of advertising executives selling the American dream from their modish Madison Avenue offices in New York is ad-man supremo and creative lead at Sterling Cooper, Don Draper (Jon Hamm). He is charismatic, capricious and handsome. In specifying the bespoke suits that Don wears as protective corporate armour, Bryant has been inspired by the suavity of archetypal matinée idol Cary Grant in the film *North by Northwest* (1959):

> 'The show is dark, and it's dramatic and it can be very sad and it's very real, and I always want to make sure that the costume design has that integrity for each of the characters.'

Don is a self-constructed myth. As Richard 'Dick' Whitman, he is the illegitimate child of a prostitute, living with his violent father and stepmother. After his father dies he moves from the family farm to a brothel ran by his stepfather, 'Uncle Mack' Johnson (Morgan Rusler). While on military service in

above Idly waiting for her first husband Don to come home, Betty (January Jones) still maintains her perfect *maquillage* and *coiffure*; she wears a circular, Sunray pleated skirt – a distant homage to the leisured, man-nered styles of Dior's New Look. In the frustrations of constraint in her gendered role as a traditional suburban housewife, Betty suffers what US feminist Betty Friedan later identified as the 'problem that has no name' in her book *The Feminine Mystique* (1963). Betty experiences the physical symptoms of psychological distress. In the final season, and following her second marriage, she enrols at college to study psychology and is seen reading Sigmund Freud's book *Dora, An Analysis of a Case of Hysteria* (1905), clearly relating the subject matter to her past experiences.

opposite The main cast members are (left to right) Pete Campbell, Joan Harris (Christina Hendricks), Roger Sterling, Peggy Olson, Don and Betty. Early in the series, Peggy and Betty wear the ultra feminine 1950s silhouette of corseted waist and full skirts as fashions continued to be influenced by Christian Dior's New Look of 1947. In the office, the men wear close-fitting suits with flat-front trousers and slim-line single-breasted jackets, a natural silhouette appropriate for a fast-paced, contemporary lifestyle.

above Peggy is the most consistent female presence in Don's life, both as a friend and as a colleague. Her wardrobe and look has evolved from pony-tailed frumpiness to her looking groomed and efficient with few wardrobe flourishes apart from favouring a pussycat bow, a female twist on the male tie. Don wears his suits as armour: he is uncomfortable when his boss suggests that he take off his jacket as 'this is a shirtsleeves office'. While others embrace new trends, his personal professional style differs only slightly in details from suit colour and tailoring to tie patterns, cufflinks and pocket handkerchiefs.

opposite left Initially seen as the 'courtesan' of the drama and latterly recast to the role of 'mother and waitress' to the advertising executives, Joan has to endure the male gaze throughout the series. As fashion moves away from the highly corseted hourglass figure of the early 1960s into A-line body-skimming shift dresses, Joan adheres to her signature style of body-enhancing garments. Although demanding recognition for her professional achievements, she also enjoys attracting male attention.

above right As aspiring actress Megan (Jessica Paré) moves to Los Angeles, Don makes the move to embrace bicoastal living. In greeting his second wife Megan at the airport, a sartorial polarity is clearly evidenced between them. She is the epitome of 1960s youthful cool with a revealing baby-blue minidress and bare legs. Don sticks to his own personal style, even wearing a fedora, which is the hat of choice for the ageing Hollywood Rat Pack. This fell out of fashion once John F. Kennedy, who disliked this accessory, was inaugurated as president in 1961.

overleaf Don's wives are in complete contrast physically and emotionally. The self-belief of former model Betty relies on her beauty and her status as an adjunct to a successful man. Megan represents the contemporary woman challenging the traditional role of the wife. She is in full-on late-1960s mode with chandelier earrings and bouffant hair – hairpieces were popular during this period to add volume and curl.

the Korean War (1950–1953), Don assumes the identity of a dead soldier, Lieutenant Donald Francis Draper (Troy Ruptash). This deception fuels his drive to succeed, a trajectory that culminates in his partnership at Sterling Cooper Draper Pryce. In the process, he leaves behind two wives and numerous other women, and neglects his children.

Don's colleagues include second-generation advertising executive and co-founder of Sterling Cooper, Roger Sterling (John Slattery), as his laid-back boss and Pete Campbell (Vincent Kartheiser) as an aspirational account executive. In keeping with the mores of the time, the group are hard-drinking, chain-smoking womanisers. Roger is also an early adopter of the fashions and excesses of the era, experimenting with hallucinogenic drugs and sporting an on-trend moustache. The female protagonist, Peggy Olson (Elisabeth Moss), has a parallel storyline to Don as she reveals a gift for copywriting, moving from secretarial duties to chief copywriter at McCann Erickson. Never fashion-forward, her advancement is marked quietly by the purchase of a skirt suit.

In the series last episode, Don leaves the office and heads for California, caught up in the hippy dream. Yet the viewer is led to believe that he returns to his old life in advertising and creates the iconic Coke advertisement from 1971, 'I'd Like to Buy the World a Coke', that ends the closing credits.

HALSTON

JERIANA SAN JUAN (2021)

above Wearing his signature tight-fitting black turtleneck – a garment associated with artists and intellectuals – Halston sits in his celestial atelier, the twenty-first floor of the Olympic Tower at 641 Fifth Avenue. The panoramic view of the Manhattan skyline includes the spires of St Patrick's Cathedral. The mirrored glass of the walls extends from floor to ceiling, reflecting the contemporary minimalism of his collections, shown to his famous clients including Elizabeth Taylor, Lauren Bacall and Liza Minnelli.

opposite above Ready to do battle at Versailles with Bobbi Mahoney (Shannan Wilson), Halston, dressed all in black, arrives at the airport with David Mahoney (Bill Pullman), Joe Eula, Elsa Peretti, Liza Minnelli and Pat Ast (Shawna Hamic). His house models Pat Cleveland (Dilone), Beverly Johnson, Karen Bjornson (Sietzka Rose) and Alva Chinn (Alanna Arrington) were known as the 'Halstonettes', and are wearing versions of the ultrasuede shirt dress. Halston was one of the few designers to use models of colour. Elsa wears a tube of lilac matte jersey.

opposite below The fashion show as seen within the context of a filmed series is an accessible and immediate way to communicate the designer's aesthetic, it also offers the possibility of a future commercial tie-in. Here, the look has all the hallmarks of the Halston brand: fluidity, drape and unconscious elegance. On the runway in his showroom, the designer lightens his customary black turtleneck with a white suit, a look first adopted by US novelist, journalist and social commentator Tom Wolfe in the early 1960s.

One of the most influential of his generation of US designers, Roy Halston Frowick is given the high-glamour biopic treatment by director Daniel Minahan, with Ryan Murphy as executive producer. Interpreting Halston's aesthetic presented New York-based costume designer Jeriana San Juan with a unique opportunity to bring his understated easy-to-wear look of unengineered sexy elegance to the small screen:

> 'It was always going to be a challenge that I had this very thin rope to walk between paying complete homage to Halston and what he did as a designer and his beautiful clothes [and] also [remaining] a storyteller as a costume designer.'

The life of Halston (Ewan McGregor) is dramatised against a backdrop of the louche, drug-fuelled excesses of the *demi-monde* in the 1970s. Initially a milliner for department store Bergdorf Goodman in New York and designer of Jacqueline Kennedy's famous pillbox hat, Halston launches his own clothing brand in 1969. His first collection fails, and it is not until he persuades *Cabaret* (1972) star Liza Minnelli (Krysta Rodriguez) to discard her 'little girl clothes' by draping her in a slither of red silk that he finds his personal aesthetic. The garments are constructed from pliable fabrics such as silk and matt jersey. His favourite fabric is an expensive fibre called ultrasuede, which he uses to make his iconic shirt dress. When Barbara 'Babe' Paley

above Elsa models a length of patterned silk dyed by Joel in his kitchen sink. Halston wields his scissors and in moments transforms it into the prototype of his best-selling kimonos. They are constructed from a single piece of fabric – with a central ovoid shape cut in the centre along the bias – folded in half to accommodate the shoulders, then folded again from the outer shoulder straight down along the grain. Both long bias edges are then finally attached and sewn together. The resulting shape, when laid flat, is a rectangle.

left Joel, an early friend of Halston's, in full mod mode, with floral shirt and heavy jewellery. His hair is cut in a moptop style exemplified by The Beatles. The white, striped suit has the hallmarks of early 1970s tailoring – influenced by the 1940s – with wide lapels on the long-line single-breasted jacket and horizontal jetted pockets.

(Regina Schneider), an influential doyenne of the New York fashion scene and former fashion editor at *Vogue*, buys the design in every colour, Halston's success is confirmed. With the assistance of his cohorts, illustrator Joe Eula (David Pittu), Joel Schumacher (Rory Culkin) and jeweller Elsa Peretti (Rebecca Dayan), Halston goes on to become one of the most powerful forces in US fashion, successfully elevating leisurewear to the level of couture.

The series follows Halston's decline into excessive drug use and a licentious lifestyle, particularly when he is introduced to the notorious Studio 54 New York nightclub by his window-dresser lover Victor Hugo (Gian Franco Rodriguez). In the drama, Halston is portrayed as a visionary who prizes ideas over financial gain. However, as the drama unfolds, the battle between the corporate world and the creative artist leaves him without control of his name and designing luggage, eyewear, carpets, various uniforms and, eventually, the Halston III range for the mid-market department store chain JCPenney. The series ends as Halston, suffering from AIDS, cruises along the Pacific coast in his Rolls-Royce convertible reminiscing about his past triumphs.

above In 1973, Halston is chosen as one of five designers alongside Bill Blass, Oscar de la Renta, Anne Klein and Stephen Burrows to represent the United States in the legendary Battle of Versailles Fashion Show featuring US and French talent at the Palace of Versailles. Halston receives a standing ovation for his collection of free-floating evening dresses. Variations on the rectangle, involving folding, wrapping and the use of the bias, are typical of the ease of Halston's style, which often deployed only a single seam in a single length of fabric.

FEUD:
BETTE AND JOAN

LOU EYRICH (2017)

Two legends of the silver screen battle for dominance in Ryan Murphy's *Feud: Bette and Joan.* The drama charts the rivalry between two-time Oscar winner Bette Davis (Susan Sarandon) and one-time Oscar winner Joan Crawford (Jessica Lange) as they seek to reignite their careers with the thriller-horror movie *What Ever Happened to Baby Jane?* (1962), based on Henry Farrell's novel of 1960 that concerns the toxic relationship between two sisters, Blanche and 'Baby Jane' Hudson.

In designing the costumes for *Feud,* the first consideration for costume designer Lou Eyrich was expressing the difference in style of the two leading protagonists, particularly their contrasting silhouettes:

'[They] were iconic real people – a ton of research was available. I read some books on them, listened to Joan Crawford's book on tape, watched a lot of videos and interviews, and both of them were on a lot of talk shows. But I didn't watch many of their old movies, because I didn't want to be influenced by those times when they were playing characters.'

Around 20 per cent of the costumes were custom-made, 40 per cent made to order, and the remaining garments were purchased or rented. Spanning from the 1930s to the 1970s, all outfits required accessories, from handbags, hats and gloves to jewellery.

above Arriving on set, Bette is smoking one of her hundred cigarettes a day. She wears a harmonious blend of red fox fur, pale orange dress, tortoiseshell belt buckle and an armful of Bakelite bangles. Made from a mixture of phenol and formaldehyde, Bakelite was patented in 1907 by Belgian chemist Leo Baekeland. The plastic was enthusiastically adopted by the jewellery industry from the 1920s to the 1940s for its range of colours and its malleable qualities.

opposite Writing under the headline 'Hedda Hopper's Hollywood' for the *Los Angeles Times,* influential gossip columnist Hedda (left) visits Joan wearing one of her signature hats. They were such a feature of her style that the Internal Revenue Service gave her a $5,000 annual tax credit for them as a work expense. Many of the hats used for the series are vintage Jack McConnell designs, custom-made by the milliner himself.

top left In *What Ever Happened to Baby Jane?*, Bette plays the deranged former child star, Baby Jane, who believes she is responsible for the accident that has rendered her sister Blanche paraplegic. Sequestered in a decaying Hollywood mansion, she torments her sister, a former film star who is now bedridden. Joan realises that Bette will steal the movie when she first sees her in her role as Baby Jane wearing grotesque make-up and an adult version of the stage clothes she wore as a child. The original costume was designed by Norma Koch, who won an Oscar for Best Costume Design for the film.

below left On location in Louisiana for their second film together, *Hush... Hush, Sweet Charlotte* (1964), Joan feels marginalised when she discovers that Bette has a close relationship with the director (again Robert Aldrich). Joan is ready for her shot in a fitted sheath dress with a green lace overlay and a deep *décolletage*. It is worn with maximum glamour, ornate jewellery and perfectly coiffed hair. More contemporary and in tune with the relaxed approach of the early 1960s, off-screen Bette favours Capri pants and a gold, loosely fitting shirt. Crawford eventually dropped out of the production.

opposite The Academy Awards ceremony in 1963 is replicated in its entirety by the costume and production team for the drama. Although Joan fails to be nominated, she secures herself a stage appearance by manipulating the other aspiring nominees to allow her to accept the award on their behalf should they win. Joan wears a dazzling, all-silver ensemble befitting her status: a heavily beaded dress that requires a corset infrastructure to take the weight, silver nail varnish and flakes of silver in her hair. The original dress was made by Edith Head, renowned lead costume designer at Paramount Pictures, as a private commission for her.

Joan's desire to retain her position as one of Hollywood's most beautiful women, with a stately demeanour, requires full-on maintenance, dresses fitted at the waist and punctilious attention to detail-matching jewellery and overdone *maquillage* with particular emphasis on her trademark eyebrows. The more she ages, the more desperately she clings to her outdated notions of glamour. Bette, never reliant on her looks for her theatrical and movie success, presents a more casual style, off duty wearing sweater sets, loose slacks with flat shoes and check shirts.

The career of both stars is on a downward trajectory, Joan has not made a film for three years when she discovers a novel she wants to adapt and realises that Bette is the only possible contender to play opposite her. During the production, Joan and Bette exchange barbed insults and feed scurrilous stories about each other to their chosen gossipmongers, Joan to Hedda Hopper (Judy Davis), Bette to Louella Parsons. The director of the picture, Robert Aldrich (Alfred Molina), fuels the stars' animosity as a

means of adding further tension to the relationship, both on and off the screen. Even though Joan instigates the project and the casting, it is Bette, not her, who is nominated for an Academy Award for best actress. Although the film is a huge box-office success, neither women receive subsequent offers of work commensurate with their talent and experience. The two stars remain unreconciled to the end of their days. On hearing of Joan's death, Bette reportedly said: 'My mother told me never to speak ill of the dead, only good. Crawford's dead? Good.'

THE DEUCE

ANNA TERRAZAS, JENNY GERING,
HANNA SHEA (2017–2019)

above Unmistakable in their dandy swagger, pimps Larry Brown (Gbenga Akinnagbe, left) and C. C. (Gary Carr) wait at the Port Authority Bus Terminal 'looking for products': young, vulnerable out-of-town girls to be recruited by them as sex workers. Regarded as the elite of the streets with their diamond studded watches, mink coats and Cadillac cars, the duo add the all-important accessories – the cane, hat and Cuban-heeled shoes – to their checked and pinstriped suits. The exaggerated lapels, flared trousers, wide ties and pointed shirt collars are a more extreme version of what was then in fashion.

opposite Hot pants (cropped, tight-fitting shorts) were a way of retaining the sexiness and freedom of the mini as skirts dropped to mid-calf at the end of the 1960s. Advertising what she is selling, and for maximum exposure, Eileen aka 'Candy' wears an unstructured, knitted halterneck bra top and leg-lengthening high-heeled platforms for her time on the streets. Newer to the game, her co-worker updates her shorts with knee-high boots and a sleeveless gilet in the new midi length.

The sleazy underworld of sex workers and their pimps in the dive bars, peep shows and detritus of the streets of midtown Manhattan is the setting for *The Deuce*, and the show's title is derived from the nickname for 42nd Street between Seventh Avenue and Eighth Avenue. Created by David Simon with writer George Pelecanos, the drama is set in the early 1970s when pornography and prostitution were becoming more widely disseminated through films such as *Midnight Cowboy* (1969), *Klute* (1971) and *Deep Throat* (1972). It chronicles the development and ultimate legalisation of the porn industry through various characters including the Brooklyn-raised twins Vincent and Frankie Martino (both played by James Franco). Frankie is a gambler and drug dealer who becomes involved in the mob, while Vincent is a well-meaning, dependable bartender.

Costume designer Anna Terrazas – followed by Jenny Gering (eight episodes) and Hanna Shea (four episodes) – was inspired, in part, by the film *The Panic in Needle Park* (1971), which follows the lives of heroin addicts, for the unglamorous look of the period:

> 'No one dressed pristine and perfect, especially these girls, so we put [cigarette burns] and dirt on the clothes and when you watch the show, you can really feel and smell what's happening in these clothes.'

She sourced vintage stores and sites for clothes from the 1970s for the series, including high-waisted jeans, platform

above Bra-less beneath her open blouse and with her kohl-rimmed eyes, blonde bubble perm and lipsticked cupid's bow, Eileen aka 'Candy' resembles the movie queens of the silent era and the liberated spirit of the 1920s, appealing to a particular sort of punter. Vincent sports a Zapata moustache popular in the 1960s, worn by the counterculture in homage to the Mexican freedom fighter Emiliano Zapata and South American revolutionary and guerrilla leader Che Guevara. Sex worker Ruby 'Thunder Thighs' (Pernell Walker) sports a printed satin bra-top dress and leopard-print faux fur coat and wears her hair in an Afro representing the natural-hair movement then prevalent.

shoes, moth-eaten fur coats and skinny-knit sweaters, all showing grime and evident signs of wear and tear. However, people have become taller and heavier since then, and the changes in body shape meant the majority of the costumes had to be made. To create authenticity, Terrazas also took inspiration from documentary video footage and books including Bob Adelman's *Gentleman of Leisure: A Year in the Life of a Pimp* (2006).

The chief protagonist in the series is Eileen 'Candy' Merrell (Maggie Gyllenhaal), who as performer, producer and director is instrumental in the transition of pornography from the city streets to the screen. As power-based transactional sex remains exploitative both on-screen and off-, she is frustrated in her endeavour to replace the male gaze with erotic films geared towards a female audience. The drama ends in the mid-1980s with the onset of AIDS and an initiative by New York mayor Ed Koch to clean up the streets. He closes the bathhouses and massage parlours in an attempt to drive the regeneration of an area ripe for development, resulting in Eileen following the porn industry

as it moves west away from New York. In Los Angeles, she builds a relationship with her mentor, fellow pornographer Harvey Wasserman (David Krumholtz).

The trashy, flashy influence of the disco era and New York's influential night club Studio 54, with its boob tubes and Spandex, is evident as the series moves from 1971 to the mid-1980s. Eileen adopts a more sophisticated version when she becomes a successful pornographer, wearing pegtop trousers worn with racerback vests and tops in soft, drape fabrics that enhance her gym-honed physique, in the new era of workouts, worn beneath big-shouldered, leather blousons.

above left Now living on the West Coast, Eileen wears all the hallmarks of mid-1980s success: the outsize tinted sunglasses, swept-back updo and statement earrings are partnered with a leather corset seamed and darted to shape. The director of eighty-nine films, Eileen is recognised in her fictional obituary in 2019 as a ground-breaking filmmaker for her art-house classic *A Pawn in Their Game*. She removed the sex scenes as Wasserman advised her to make the movie more mainstream.

above right Abigail 'Abby' Parker (Margarita Levieva), the archetypal 1970s student in high-waist, flared jeans, shrunken sweater and hippy hair, combines her college activities with sex working. Army surplus clothing appealed to both students and hippies, because it was cheap and also in ironic recognition of the Vietnam War (1955–1975). When her relationship with Vincent ends, he gives her the bar, which she then passes on to her friend Loretta (Sepideh Moafi), preferring to resume her education and study law.

THE SERPENT

RACHEL WALSH, ADAM HOWE (2021)

above Tailored trouser suits for women were first intro-duced by Parisian couturier Yves Saint Laurent in 1966 at a time when formal trousers were still forbidden for women in various institutions, restaurants and the work-place. Marie-Andrée represents the nascent women's movement in a version that is cut from an original Yves Saint Laurent block from the 1970s. The introduction of waist darts and the curved lapels emphasise the femi-nine shape of the jacket which is worn with high-waisted, flat-front trousers. Her gaze is hidden behind Cartier sunglasses, which are replicas of the face-shading originals. Charles' powder-blue suit is cut from a 1970s pattern block sourced from British fashion house DAKS.

opposite left The late 1960s and early 1970s saw a plethora of print and pattern in fashion, eagerly adopted by the hippy culture. Marie-Andrée's sleeve-less top features a polychromatic geometric design. The predatory Charles displays an insouciant chic in low-rise, flat-fronted trousers and a fitted shirt, worn with turned-back cuffs and a fashionable wide spread collar. He wears aviator-style glasses, which were first launched in 1935 to protect pilots' eyes from the cold air and glare of the cockpit. They became popular for civilian use in the 1970s.

The 1970s hippy dream of freedom to roam the world with impunity is shattered in the thriller *The Serpent* written by Richard Warlow and Toby Finlay, based on the real-life story of Frenchman Charles Sobhraj (Tahar Rahim), a predatory serial killer who drugs and tortures at least a dozen victims throughout Thailand, India and Nepal. It is the height of the counterculture, an opportunity for costume designers Rachel Walsh and Adam Howe, to exploit a 1970s aesthetic of hippy kaftans and flared jeans juxtaposed with sharp 1970s tailoring enjoyed by the lead protagonist Charles. Walsh is clear about that the need not to exaggerate or distort the costumes of the era:

'There's a fine line between flower power and Austin Powers. We wanted the characters to look alive and vibrant, without becoming caricatures.'

To this end, she referenced archive issues of *Vogue* magazine, taking apart vintage jeans, blouses and dresses and recon-structing them to fit Marie-Andrée Leclerc (Jenna Coleman), always with an eye to contemporary style icons such as the waifish Jane Birkin and trouser-suited Bianca Jagger.

Born in Saigon to an Indian father and a Vietnamese mother, Charles, nicknamed 'the Serpent' for his snakelike avoidance of capture, is quick to capitalise on the weak-ness of travellers adrift in a strange land who are often drug-addled, vulnerable and easily exploited. The sociopath befriends them in the guise of being helpful. Charles first meets his girlfriend Marie-Andrée in Kashmir while she is on holiday. Although she appears shy and has made no attempt with her appearance, wearing dowdy, overlarge T-shirts and with her hair pulled back, he sees her potential for manipulation. Under his attentions, she blossoms into an elegant and sophisticated young women, successfully emulating the images of the models she sees in the many fashion magazines she devours endlessly. Marie-Andrée and Charles are eager to appear as a glamorous couple, the easier to lull unsuspecting victims. Marie-Andrée is in thrall to her boyfriend, enabling him to entice backpackers to his house in Bangkok, a scene of endless drink and drug-fuelled parties. Although apparently unquestioning of the victims' ultimate fate, she is fully cognisant of the effect of the drugged drinks she gives them. The two of them live off the traveller's cheques of their victims, doctoring their passports to enable them to move from country to country and evade capture.

The narrative of the drama is fragmented, with flash-backs in time and place between Charles, his many victims and Herman Knippenberg (Billy Howle), a junior diplomat from the Netherlands, who jeopardises his career and his marriage as he becomes obsessed with tracking down Charles after the murder of a young Dutch couple. With the hippies dismissed by the authorities as 'work-shy hobos' and 'long hairs', they are reluctant to help until Herman eventually attracts the attention of Interpol by an article he writes for the *Bangkok Post*, resulting in an international warrant for their arrest. A game of cat and mouse follows, with Charles finally interred in a Nepali jail, where he remains, and Marie-Andrée, the chief witness against him, allowed to return to Canada after her diagnosis of a terminal illness.

above Marie-Andrée wears a loose unstructured top in a surface pattern redolent of the prints designed by the Italian 'Prince of Prints', Emilio Pucci. He designed for the newly mobile 'beautiful people' such as Jacqueline Kennedy Onassis and Bianca Jagger. His signature style was abstract, non-figurative form in psychedelic swirls of dazzling colour.

IT'S A SIN

IAN FULCHER (2021)

above 'Not a housewarming, we are going to have a party every night,' says Ritchie on moving into the Pink Palace, so called because of the long-held association between the shade and homosexuality, and also referring to the camp pink mug sent by his mother. To raise awareness of the AIDS crisis, the organisation ACT-UP decided to use the pink-triangle badge as a symbol of its campaign. As an act of reclamation, this was an inversion of an historic precedent from the 1930s when people, stigmatised as homosexual, were forced by the Nazi regime to wear a pink triangle symbol. The badge continues to be worn as a sign of support for the LGBTQ+ community. The dress code for the house party makes faint reference to the workwear and rodeo tropes of denim and plaid shirts made global by the Village People group at the beginning of the 1980s.

opposite Roscoe is the most flamboyant of the group wearing crudely knitted string vests with high-waisted, acid-washed jeans, accessorised with chains, chokers and steel-capped black boots. It is a look fusing elements of the Seditionaries line by British designer Vivienne Westwood with the stock signifiers of S&M and the Village People. He can also adopt a chameleon quality as he sets aside his post-punk accoutrements, donning a camouflage of traditionally tailored suits in grey and navy when in a relationship with the closeted Conservative MP Arthur Garrison (Stephen Fry).

Bringing together a group of young people under one roof is a familiar device, witness *Friends* (1994–2004) or *This Life* (1996–1997). The format provides a setting for the intertwined lives and plot development of a small cast of characters. In the miniseries *It's a Sin,* created and written by Russell T. Davies, a distinction lies in the growing sense of foreboding even at the outset of the opening episode. Beginning in 1981, the drama celebrates a brief period of time when young gay men could explore their sexuality before the onset of AIDS.

British costume designer Ian Fulcher researched contemporary images from the 1980s for the drama, sourcing vintage fabrics and garments from eBay, Beyond Retro, Rokit and secondhand shops throughout the northwest of England, where the drama series was shot, to clothe the group of friends. In a post-punk era, their clothes remain believable and unremarkable, untouched by the conspicuous narcissism and historical appropriation of the New Romantics youth culture of the early 1980s that dominated London's LGBTQ+ social scene. As Fulcher confirms:

'Groups of people who went places together dressed the same... they'd know that they could recognise someone from their tribe based on their dress code.'

The diverse characters sharing the flat are the flamboyant Roscoe Babatunde (Omari Douglas), and the shy, diffident Colin Morris-Jones (Callum Scott Howells), who

top left Colin (right) moves to London to undertake his training in the gentlemen's bespoke trade of Savile Row. Shy and naive, he is unworldly without connection to the gay community until he meets his urbane colleague Henry Coltrane (Neil Patrick Harris), who takes him to his home to meet his live-in male partner. Although wearing a traditional Savile Row three-piece suit, Henry sports discreet eccentricities such as the pocket square carefully positioned into three interlocking triangles and a paisley tie, anchored with a gold tiepin.

centre left Roscoe startles his strict, religious family, who are dully besuited with collar and tie, by quickly changing from a check shirt and hoodie into the sunburst vision of a 1960s go-go dancer in miniskirt, fringed satin turban and crop top. He tells his family he is leaving and declares unequivocally: 'I'll be staying at 23 Piss Off Avenue, London, W Fuck.' He then races out of the front door to join his friends in the Pink Palace.

below left Ritchie – dressed for action – jumps on a policeman in a confrontation at a protest rally. His chosen battledress outfit is a 1980s favourite: double denim, comprising a fur-collared Wrangler Sherpa jacket and jeans, turned up over white high-tops for a quick getaway.

leaves the Welsh valleys to work in a men's outfitters on Savile Row. They are joined as flatmates by drama students Ritchie Tozer (Olly Alexander) and his friend-with-benefits Ash Mukherjee (Nathaniel Curtis). Jill Baxter (Lydia West) is the matriarch of the group, always clothed in soft, comforting textures, such as mohair sweaters or towelling robes.

In a joyful celebration of freedom and unfettered erotic impulses, they leave behind the restrictions of suburbia and family life to congregate in the pubs and clubs of the big city, while defying the rhetoric of condemnation from a prejudiced and gay-averse society. They lead their lives against the backdrop of the implementation of the Section 28 legislation in 1988 by Margaret Thatcher's Conservative government, which prohibited the 'promotion of homosexuality' by local authorities.

Apart from Jill, the friends are at first unaware and then dismissive of the threat of the burgeoning AIDS epidemic.

She asks Colin to buy any available literature on the subject when he makes a trip to New York. She attempts to warn the group of the dangers inherent in their behaviour, but in a montage of nightclub scenes, Ritchie recites to camera his list of reasons why practising safe sex would compromise his desire for untrammelled sexual freedom: 'It's a racket, it's a moneymaking scheme for drugs companies... They want to scare us and stop us having sex and make us really boring basically because they can't get laid.'

Harrowing scenes unfold in various hospital wards – the lab coats worn by the doctors in the AIDS clinic are original, delivered in packaging complete with a '1982 certified' stamp. Ritchie, too, falls victim, returning to his family home on the Isle of Wight, where his mother refuses to allow any of his friends to visit. As he lies on his death-bed, reflecting on the past few years, he has no regrets: 'That's what people will forget – that it was all so much fun.'

above The five friends (left to right) Ash, Colin, Roscoe, Jill and Ritchie pose, happy together in the park. Apart from Roscoe's studded leather choker and Neville Brody-inspired graphic T-shirt, the flatmates have disparate, low-key looks. Distressed and double denim make connection with the early style of pop stars Madonna and Wham!, while turned-back sleeves recall the *Michael Jackson: Thriller* (1983) music video. Colin is distinctly non-metropolitan in his dress and personal style; his mail-order ski jacket is ardently provincial sports casual.

There are both advantages and challenges in designing the costumes for any TV series based in the present. A contemporary drama has the potential to have a cast dressed in clothes that may be immediately available through retail outlets or, when rapidly recycled, more economically sourced through eBay. A costume designer is able to exploit the general market awareness of an audience to establish aspects of the character's profile. From indicating the well-heeled and self-indulgent to signalling poverty and self-doubt, or even a simple enjoyment in fashion, clothes are highly legible within the span of their currency.

The aim of designers is twofold: to see at first hand which influences might mature into solid significance, and to avoid catching the tailcoats of an ephemeral trend that would render the series out of date even before general release. The extended production time from pilot to release of any series set in the present can put the intended impact of on-trend, short-wave fashion in jeopardy. By a strange digital osmosis, some fashion pieces gain a commercial afterlife from being worn on screen and shopped online through specialist channels and influencers.

One of the series keenly featured on 'as worn on TV' shopping sites is *Inventing Anna* (see p 198). The real-life saga of an extreme wannabe, Anna Soronkin (aka Anna Delvey) played by Julia Garner, whose endless upwardly mobile deceits are effected with the aid of an ill-gotten luxe wardrobe. For the series, the designer was able to secure 3,000 contemporary outfits to depict Anna forging her future in the glossy precincts of high culture and high fashion.

Actors have always embraced the alchemical power of costume within the imperative of character projection. It is far from unusual for designers to work hand in hand with cast members – particularly in contemporary series – to find clothes that amplify nuances of their role. Producers and directors – key agents in a series ensemble – also share costume ideas with the designers. This collaborative

above Lyn Paolo, costume designer for *Inventing Anna*, was tasked with mirroring the unlikely but true narrative arc of Anna Delvey (aka Anna Soronkin) in her career as a well-heeled fraudster, disguised in luxury brands. Shown maturing from her days as a London fashion student, Anna is described as having become a native, front-row-grade, fashion persona. In a celebratory mood, Anna wears the Emilia dress in gunmetal by Dress the Population.

approach strengthens in line with the extent that the series is renewed, giving opportunity for character evolution expressed in wardrobe choices over a time span.

Lena Dunham, creator, writer and protagonist actor in *Girls* (see p 192), gave her designer, Jennifer Rogien, a clear and powerful brief of prioritising believability over making the characters look good. After four seasons of fashion *faux pas* Hannah Horvath discovers a more mature personal style in the safety zone of the A-line, abandoning her previous ill-fitting *déshabillé*. In league with the designer, she develops through an early dependency on don't-look-at-me-like-that looks to arrive at an equilibrium of self-confidence in a vintage – $30 – Etsy-sourced, 1960s shift dress for her role as a university lecturer. Through the fashion choices for her role as Hannah, Dunham was able to semaphore the tagline for the series: 'Living the dream. One mistake at a time.'

THE NIGHT MANAGER

SIGNE SEJLUND (2016)

above On duty at the Nefertiti Hotel in Cairo, Jonathan exudes efficiency and untrammelled handsomeness in his hotel uniform: a slimline Garda suit by British high-end brand Reiss. The suit expresses his identity as a manager, unobtrusive yet elegant, the perfect English gentleman. Styled with a single button-fastening, peaked lapels and four functioning buttons at the cuff, it is worn with a matching waistcoat. The flat-front trousers have pressed, centre creases.

opposite Jed is a former New York model whom Richard picked up from the Upper East Side. For him, she is a willowy, blonde status symbol unencumbered by the child she has left behind with her mother. Her cropped, side-parted hair is shorn at the neck elongating her 6-foot 2-inch frame, which is usually draped in pastel, neoclassical layers. The only evidence of Richard's wealth is the barely visible IWC Spitfire pilot's watch in gold that he wears with a standard, creased linen shirt and chinos.

British writer John le Carré's espionage thriller *The Night Manager* (1993) was set in the early 1990s but this was changed to the early 2010s for the six-part TV miniseries to encompass the contemporary uprisings across the Arab world. Sumptuously shot by Danish director Susanne Bier, the drama features a plethora of luxurious foreign hotels, sunrise over the Alps, Egyptian pyramids at sunset, speedboats cutting a curve through a cerulean sea and other visual fireworks.

The immaculately suited Jonathan Pine (Tom Hiddleston), a veteran of the Iraq War (2003–2011), is the eponymous manager of the Nefertiti Hotel in Cairo during the Egyptian Revolution of 2011. When a beautiful guest, Sophie Alekan (Aure Atika), requests to copy some documents, she confides that they contain evidence of a negotiation conducted by her boyfriend Freddie Hamid (David Avery) to purchase an arsenal of weapons from a suave arms dealer, Richard Roper (Hugh Laurie), who has the covert backing of the Whitehall political establishment to sell arms to the embattled developing nations. Jonathan shares the documents with British intelligence and becomes romantically involved with Sophie. After she is murdered, he moves to Switzerland to become the night manager at the Meisters Hotel, Zermatt. Four years later, he encounters Richard there, now with his beautiful girlfriend Jemima 'Jed' Marshall (Elizabeth Debicki).

top left Richard, Jed and assorted henchmen arrive by helicopter at the luxurious Meisters Hotel to be greeted by Jonathan. Beneath the striped, dyed fur coat, Jed wears a taupe sleeveless sweater dress from London store Selfridges, which she removes in one swift, sensuous movement before taking a bath in front of Richard and his entourage.

centre left Sent undercover as 'Jack Linden' to the Devon coast to provide a convincing backstory as a renegade soldier and drugs dealer, Jonathan confirms his alpha-male credentials. He is booted and leather-suited in a Matchless London leather jacket, hoodie and J Brand Kane jeans. Astride a Triumph Thruxton 900 motorcycle, Jonathan stares challengingly into the future through his sunglasses from Under Armour.

below left While on Majorca, Jonathan and Jed head to the beach and as he asks what she knows of Richard's business. 'Buying and selling,' she shrugs, and invites him to swim with her. She displays an air of drifting indolence, her garments reflecting her fluid, amorphous role, willing to adapt to wherever Richard might take her, and with no questions asked about the source of his wealth. Later, she unties the bow at the neck of her dress, allowing it to float to her feet in a cloud of ice-blue silk chiffon before she wades out to sea, naked, initiating their mutual attraction.

opposite On the terrace of the luxurious converted fort on the island of Majorca, Jonathan, now known as 'Andrew Birch' is wearing one of the bespoke suits provided by his boss and is confident and at ease in his new role as Richard's favourite henchman. Jed stands with her habitual passivity, clothed in transparent layers. The bodice of the dress, split to the waist, is threaded through a simple tie that fastens at the back of the neck.

Danish costume designer Signe Sejlund clothes the long, lissom form of Jed as the 'trophy wife' in a series of floating, columnar dresses seemingly devoid of zips, buttons or fastenings of any type, allowing her proprietorial husband instant access to her body. She expresses a floating lassitude in her draped passivity:

> 'I had to discard a lot of clothes I brought to the fitting because although they would have been full length on a normal person, on Elizabeth they came just below her knee.'

Following the meeting, and intent on avenging Sophie's death, Jonathan is contacted by British intelligence officer Angela Burr (Olivia Colman), who enlists him to provide evidence of Richard's activities. After working on a backstory, Angela sends Jonathan to Majorca, Spain, to work undercover as 'Thomas Quince'. There he foils the fake kidnap attempt of Richard's son, which was set up by Angela. In gratitude, Richard invites him to the family's luxurious compound, a converted fort. He becomes one of

Richard's trusted henchman, who gives him a new identity as 'Andrew Birch'. Jonathan infiltrates Richard's organisation to the point of being invaluable to the success of an operation involving seven British and US companies selling arms to Lebanon. Jonathan's acceptance of the role is marked by a new wardrobe commensurate with his new status: a series of made-to-measure suits in Prince of Wales check and birdseye cloth from London tailor Thom Sweeney. They mark his rite of passage and give him credibility as a high-flying banker. Murder and mayhem follow, until Richard's deal is thwarted.

above The firm's managing partner Jessica (far left) is flanked by other members of the team (Louis, Rachel, Harvey and Mike). Jessica favours structured tailoring such as this close-fitting skirt suit. Constantly besieged by aspirants to her position, Jessica has to exude power and authority through her clothes, which must be sufficiently high-status to impress clients, yet seductive enough to be persuasive. Spike heels are the inevitable accessory.

above Wearing a classic sexy-but-covered-up look, office paralegal Rachel – I'm really pretty but I'm also good at my job – is the best researcher in the firm and has her own office. She wears the archetypal pencil skirt – first introduced by Christian Dior in 1954 – cut high in the waist to emphasise the length of her legs, and narrowing towards the knees to accentuate her curves. A crisp, classic white shirt contrasts with the lace fabric of the light blue Burberry Prorsum skirt, which provides a more businesslike aesthetic.

opposite below The designer gives Harvey a suit in keeping with his position, with additional details such as a ticket pocket, in addition to a wider tie with a bigger knot. Harvey points out to his subordinate that sartorial choices are paramount in projecting the right image for the firm – he is dressed, in the main, by Tom Ford – hence his instruction to Mike: 'Go to my suit guy and spend some money.'

SUITS

JOLIE ANDREATTA, JORDANNA FINEBERG
(2011–2019)

According to US historian Anne Hollander's *Sex and Suits: the Evolution of Modern Dress* (2016), a man in a suit is visibly humming with the potential for action and an inner energy. This is true of the lead protagonists in Aaron Korsh's *Suits*, a formulaic, slick legal drama set in the high-stakes world of the US corporate law firm Pearson Hardman. Over the series, new styles are constantly added to keep abreast of trends in menswear, with the men moving away from traditional pinstripes to fabrics such as worsted Venetian cloth that convey status to the viewer. Costume designer Jolie Andreatta confirms this:

> '*Suits are like medieval suits of armour. [They] tell us who the person is, what kind of background [they come from], what kind of status they have.*'

The series begins when alpha attorney Harvey Specter (Gabriel Macht) is told to hire a trainee. Bored with interviewing a queue of lookalike Harvard graduates, he employs a university dropout with an eidetic memory, Mike Ross (Patrick J. Adams), as his new associate. Mike's lack of qualifications must remain secret from the other members of the firm, which drives the plot forwards and provides many tense moments as he attempts to cover up the shortfall in his knowledge by deploying his phenomenal photographic memory. Their colleagues include senior partner Jessica Pearson (Gina Torres), dressed for success in Tom Ford, Balenciaga, The Row and Chanel; devious and ambitious junior partner Louis Litt (Rick Hoffman); and Specter's wisecracking assistant Donna Paulsen (Sarah Rafferty), whose body-con dresses assert her role as a sexy and super-efficient secretary. Harvey alternates between chastising the new recruit for his failures and setting him seemingly impossible tasks. Mike is helped by researcher, Rachel Zane (Meghan Markle), and the couple go on to develop a romantic relationship. Costume designer Jordanna Fineberg was responsible for the final sixteen episodes.

above The group of friends (left to right) Marnie, Jessa, Hannah and Shoshanna ruminate on a park bench. Marnie makes sophisticated choices intended to make the most appropriate impact, shopping from high-end department stores such as Lord & Taylor and Blooming-dale's. Jessa, Hannah and Shoshanna are limited by budget constraints, choosing clothes from vintage stores and mass-market, high-street shops. Hannah dresses as if she has picked up her clothes from a pile left on the floor the night before. She wears a dispiriting combination of grey tights worn under open-toed shoes, a mustard miniskirt and an unironed plaid shirt.

above Trying to convince the other nannies at the park to unionise, Jessa loses sight of the children. For her day job she wears a selection of disparate garments entirely impractical for an afternoon at the park: a teal velvet, cowl-necked top and wide-legged, printed palazzo trousers worn with red, high-wedge sandals with a matching red studded-and-pleated bag.

GIRLS

JENNIFER ROGIEN (2012–2017)

'I am busy trying to become who I am,' says the narcissistic, entitled Hannah Horvath to her long-suffering parents, on their request that she should get a job, two years after she has left college. Created by activist, author and significant social-media presence Lena Dunham, the transgressive and boundary-breaking comedy drama *Girls* features four millennials based in Brooklyn, New York: Hannah (Lena Dunham), Jessa Johansson (Jemima Kirke), Marnie Michaels (Allison Williams) and Shoshanna Shapiro (Zosia Mamet). Working as an unpaid intern, Hannah has aspirations to become a voice, if not the voice of her generation. The British Jessa, having no such inclinations and following her sojourn in various foreign countries, moves into the downtown Manhattan apartment of her student cousin Shoshanna and becomes a babysitter.

Although the *Girls* pilot explicitly references HBO's previous series about the lives and loves of a quartet of New York women, *Sex and the City* (1998–2004), *Girls* is not like its predecessor. It is predicated on a more mundane approach that includes untidy, cramped apartments, insecure jobs, disastrous sexual encounters and, significantly, less aspirational high fashion. Costume designer Jennifer Rogien features only clothes that look real and believable, chosen for an assortment of characters and body types:

'One [has] to really trust the creator of the characters. In this case, Lena and Jenni [Konner] created

previous Hannah, comfortable in her ill-fitting shorts and a blouse without shape or structure spots Shoshanna, Jessa and Marnie selling off their unwanted clothes, handbags, scarves and household items on the steps of the Maiden's Milk Vintage Boutique. Wearing vintage 1970s-inspired clothes, Shoshanna is in a Raschel-knit sweater and Jessa in a floral, mid-calf dress reminiscent of the aesthetic of English designer Ossie Clark – they complete the look with platform shoes.

top left Jessa returns from her travels abroad with a Louis Vuitton suitcase containing an eclectic array of clothes amassed from foreign flea markets. She wears a grey-felt trilby worn on the back of the head and an outsize polka-dot scarf and velvet coat. Her avant-garde approach to fashion includes an impervious attitude to what is appropriate – on another occasion she wears a see-through, white-lace dress over a pink bikini when babysitting.

centre left At a warehouse party, Hannah is in one of her many frumpy cardigans, a crumpled skirt and a baggy striped top. Shoshanna takes crack cocaine for the first time, eventually leaving the party and discarding her sequinned skirt as she runs half-naked down the street. Jessa wears a black-feather jacket described as 'wear-able taxidermy', accessorised with accoutrements from her global travels, including a heavy turquoise necklace.

below left In keeping with her hippy credentials, Jessa wears a fluid kimono in a pink-on-pale-blue, floral all-over print tied at the waist. Hannah's striped dress is worn with her customary cardigan and features a short bodice with the waist positioned at the widest part of the torso, creating an unflattering line – a silhouette that recurs throughout her wardrobe.

opposite After four seasons of fashion *faux pas*, the writer and key protagonist in *Girls*, Hannah, discovers a more mature personal style in the safety zone of the A-line. In league with designer Rogien, Hannah has developed through an early dependency on 'don't-look-at-me-like-that' looks, arriving at an equilibrium of self-confidence in this vintage 1960s shift dress sourced for $30 from Etsy.

Mistakes are the portals of discovery. James Joyce

these characters and created these stories. We made a lot of costume choices that weren't conventional and weren't what were considered normal for television, and it was amazing to be able to make those choices in the creative space that Girls had... Deliberately going against everyone on the show looking great all the time was, in retrospect, groundbreaking.'

Hannah has an unabashed confidence in her body. She is sometimes naked, usually unkempt, and wears droopy side seams and tie-dye 'short-eralls' – a cross between shorts and overalls – and ill-fitting clothes. However, a stint at upmarket magazine GQ results in a less dishevelled appearance.

Marnie is an elegant counterpoint to the messy Hannah, dressing for her role as an assistant in an art gallery. At one point she is asked if she is 'one of those housewives or something?' referring to a reality TV series featuring high-maintenance women. She is careful to choose clothes that are appropriate to the event or to attract a particular man, although her look becomes more relaxed as she embraces a career as a singer–songwriter.

The evolution of character through clothes is most evident in the progression of Jessa from hippy-esque vintage velvets and transparent lace dresses to tailored jackets and skirt suits. The youngest of the group, Shoshanna, originally seen in pastel Juicy Couture tracksuits, embraces an idiosyncratic Tokyo street style when later working as an assistant manager of a cat café.

As the drama progresses, the group of friends bicker, steal each other's boyfriends, take various drugs, make some seriously bad life choices, marry, divorce, abandon a series of jobs before finally dispersing in different directions. Hannah is pregnant and about to go off to teach at a liberal-arts school upstate; Shoshanna is engaged and entering a new social circle; and Marnie leaves her drug-addicted husband and musical partner. Admitting their solipsism, Shoshanna sums up the friends' relationship: 'We can't hang out together anymore because we cannot be in the same room without one of us making it completely and entirely about ourselves.'

INVENTING ANNA

LAURA FRECON, LYN PAOLO (2022)

Posing as a German trustafarian with a $67 million inheritance, the eponymous protagonist/lead swindles friends, banks, art dealers, real-estate developers and celebrity hoteliers out of thousands of dollars. *Inventing Anna* is created by Shonda Rhimes, it is based on an article by US journalist Jessica Pressler published in *New York Magazine* in 2018, 'Maybe She Had So Much Money She Just Lost Track of It. How an Aspiring "It" Girl Tricked New York's Party People – and Its Banks', which chronicles the unusual rise of Anna 'Delvey' Sorokin.

Charismatic and convincing, Anna Delvey (Julia Garner) – real name 'Anna Sorokin', born to a middle-class Russian family – has a grand plan to open a visual-arts centre, the Anna Delvey Foundation on Park Avenue South, New York, making her 'the gatekeeper of the global art world'. While attempting to procure loans for this enterprise, she lives in five-star hotels or sponges off rich friends, who do not bother to check their credit-card details when Anna includes her couture alongside their takeaway lunches. When staying in the apartment of socialite Nora Radford (Kate Burton) – a fictional character loosely based on a real person – Anna uses her Bergdorf Goodman account to purchase an exorbitant number of high-end label items, leaving her host to pay the bill of $400,000. Her imperious manner, huge tips to hotel staff, a wardrobe comprising couture, an array of Hermès bags and a continuous stream

above Not yet confident in her fashion choices, Anna wears a label-heavy wardrobe: a Burberry coat, Gucci bag, Dior scarf and espadrilles. Committing the sartorial sin of matchy-matchy (a mode of dressing that is excessively colour-coordinated), she carries the naval theme throughout her outfit with side-buttoned, wide-legged trousers and a double-breasted reefer (a coat with origins in the British Navy, worn by sailors whose job it was to reef the sails).

opposite Anna's boyfriend Chase Sikorski (Saamer Usmani) wants to fund his company Wake. At his suggestion, the two invite themselves onto a friend's yacht moored off Ibiza in the hope of finding an investor on-board. Anna wears a much-admired, boat-necked, body-skimming dress by Alexander McQueen. In a Grace Kelly moment, she wears outsize sunglasses with a trailing scarf designed by costumer Lyn Paolo. Both were favoured accessories of the late style icon, who was renowned for her impeccable taste and beauty, and whom Anna desires to emulate.

top left From gauche beginnings, Anna realises that she needs to curate a more sophisticated wardrobe to transform herself into a major player, dyeing her blonde hair dark auburn and sporting black-framed glasses. She wears a coat by Dries van Noten and purloins a private plane to travel to the annual shareholder meeting of business magnate Warren Buffett's company Berkshire Hathaway, in Omaha, Nebraska.

centre left Anna takes her friends to see her putative arts centre at the Church Missions House at 281 Park Avenue South. She dons her favourite label, Dries van Noten, with a floral jacquard crimson and black coat worn with a black frame, top-handle Gucci bag. Gratify-ingly impressed are celebrity trainer and life coach Kacy (far left) in a black-leather trench; Rachel (second left), who has neither the budget nor the desire for high-end fashion; and aspiring filmmaker and hotel concierge Neff (right) in an embroidered coat and print top.

below left During her trial, Anna continues to curate her own style, refusing to appear in the clothes offered by the court, instead hiring celebrity stylist Natasha Lucas (Shannon Thornton) at $12,000 a day. Anna emphasises that 'the back shouldn't be an afterthought, that's what the photographers will see'. She has an unexplained and enduring attachment to a black-velvet ribbon choker, which she wears here with a black-chiffon Michael Kors dress.

opposite Wearing a rococo-patterned Dolce & Gabbana coat, Anna is caught on Instagram when she is intro-duced as her mentor Nora's new protégée at a fundraiser. Nora displays inimitable style in a cashmere cape by French luxury brand Celine, caught at the neck with a nineteenth-century style jewelled clasp, accessorised with a crane brooch and earrings by Oscar de la Renta.

of Instagram selfies of her enjoying the high life make her a convincing candidate for a loan of $40 million.

Costume designers Lyn Paolo and Laura Frecon were able to access Delvey's Instagram account to achieve verisimilitude, as well as approaching brands, including Prada, Dolce & Gabbana, Michael Kors, Valentino, Balenciaga and Rick Owens, for the exact garments worn by Anna. Paolo says they also had many discussions with Pressler:

> 'Jessica was invaluable to the research – even down to what Anna wore when she was arrested (Chanel flats). We did so much research just trying to figure out who she was. But I think that's the whole point of the show – nobody really knows who Anna is.'

Anna's mentor Nora remains loyal to the old favourites of New York's fashion elite, Oscar de la Renta and Carolina Herrera. With her perfectly constructed couture, Nora gives Anna a masterclass in personal style that she is all too willing to embrace.

Once Anna has exhausted all potential sources of income, she flees to Los Angeles, fakes a suicide and signs herself in for rehab. There, she is arrested for fraud by the police, who have been tipped off by her friend Rachel (Katie Lowes), who is threatened with joblessness and homelessness after a credit-card fraud and a $62,000 bill following what was supposed to be an all-expenses-paid trip to Morocco.

While Anna is awaiting trial in Rikers Island prison, journalist Vivian Kent (Anna Chlumsky), who is based on Pressler, interviews Anna's many victims. They range from her personal trainer Kacy Duke (Laverne Cox) to Neff (Alexis Floyd), the trusting concierge at her hotel, who is instrumental in getting Anna on the all-important guest lists of New York's elite. Most of the latter are initially reluctant to talk because they are too embarrassed to admit to their gullibility. In 2019, Anna is convicted on eight charges including attempted grand larceny, grand larceny in the second degree and theft of services. She is sentenced to four to twelve years in prison. Updates on the screen reveal that, in real life, Sorokin was released in 2021 but arrested a month later for overstaying her visa.

above New York luxury brand The Blonds is renowned for its fashion-fantasy performance pieces inspired by the city's nightlife culture and places the corset at the centre of every collection. Cookie arrives at Leviticus, a club owned by Lucious, in a rigid, woven corset with separate high-collared yoke and cuffs that is a look deliberately redolent of Tina Turner as Aunty Entity in *Mad Max Beyond Thunderdome* (1985).

opposite Cookie visits Lucious in jail. She chooses to dress down for the occasion in a collarless, Chanel-style Moschino jacket constructed from patchwork denim and a chunky Kenneth Jay Lane necklace, and carries a Christian Louboutin bag. Lucious has been imprisoned for killing Cookie's cousin, his former employee Bunkie Williams (Antoine McKay), and wears a jumpsuit from the New York State Department of Corrections and Community Supervision.

EMPIRE

PAOLO NIEDDU (2015–2020)

With all the glitz and glamour of a *Dynasty* (1981–1989) for the 2020s, with the fabulous fashions to match, the musical drama *Empire,* created by Danny Strong and Lee Daniels, features a familiar plot line – William Shakespeare's *King Lear* (1606) – as to who gets to inherit the family business when the founder is diagnosed with a terminal medical condition. The head of Empire Entertainment, a hip-hop music and entertainment company, Lucious Lyon (Terrence Howard) – 'I started selling drugs when I was nine years old in Philadelphia, music saved me' – is head of Empire Entertainment, a hip-hop music and entertainment company founded on the drug money made by his ex-wife Cookie (Taraji P. Henson), for which she was imprisoned for seventeen years. On her release, she finds that the company is about to go public on the New York Stock Exchange and immediately demands her share of the business.

In keeping with Cookie's fierce desire for power, costume designer Paolo Nieddu, together with Rita McGhee, curates for Cookie a variety of body-con animal print garments from Italian designer Roberto Cavalli, including designs featuring the spotted coat of the female leopard – the female being the most savage fighter – perceived as representing the archetypal *femme fatale*. This, coupled with her lavish use of polychromatic furs from Fendi and thigh-high, python stiletto boots, makes her an intimidating aggressor when

top left Cookie's son Hakeem (right), the heir apparent to the business, has inherited his mother's predilection for brands and bling – Moschino trousers and gold bomber jacket, heavy chains and outsize diamond ear studs. Lucious (left) is rarely seen without a paisley or print foulard worn as a cravat, expressing his desire to be perceived as a gentleman.

centre left Cookie organises a 'Free Lucious' concert. Dressed in a gorilla suit, she descends to the stage in a cage and then disrobes to expose her diamond-mesh-and-feather green dress to the cheers of the crowd. In the audience is André Leon Talley (playing himself), who was then editor-at-large of *Vogue* magazine. She is deflated when he looks her up and down then dismisses her, saying: 'Gucci? Last season.'

below left Cookie returns to Empire Entertainment as co-CEO and head of artists and repertoire. She and Lucious are eager to appear together as a successful couple once more. Cookie is ghetto-fabulous in a silver lamé halterneck dress with butterfly wings. The drug dealer turned rapper turned ultra-rich record mogul is wearing a bronze velvet jacket with one of his signature scarves loose, rather than tucked into his collar, which is evidence of his more relaxed attitude to life now that he now knows he was misdiagnosed with ALS and is suffering instead from myasthenia gravis, a condition that does not compromise life expectancy.

opposite Wearing silver fox and a sequinned silver shift dress, supermodel Naomi Campbell as British fashion designer Camilla Marks-Whiteman appears as Hakeem's 'side piece' for the first time as his more mature partner at the White Party Foundation. Following the series, Campbell's Marc Bouwer couture minidress was auctioned with all proceeds going to her Fashion For Relief charity.

fighting for her own and her children's future. Cookie's high-end wardrobe includes designers such as Moschino, Balmain, Derek Lam, Gucci, Emanuel Ungaro and Givenchy, all accessorised with a plethora of Judith Leiber bags – unless she needs 'to carry' (a gun), when only a Chanel will do. Her killer spike heels are by Paul Andrew, Jimmy Choo and Manolo Blahnik. Adorned with outsize earrings and chunky necklaces by jewellery designers such as Kimberly McDonald and Kenneth Jay Lane, she sports a Bulgari Serpenti watch in rose gold with diamonds. Her flamboyant look gains her a fictional following of 3.3 million on social media.

The head of the family, Lucious must choose which of his three sons he should groom to take over as CEO on his anticipated demise: the eldest son bipolar Andre (Trai Byers) married to Rhonda (Kaitlin Doubleday), entitled bad-boy rap starlet Hakeem (Bryshere Y. Gray) or unassuming, gay singer-songwriter Jamal (Jussie Smollett). All three are dressed as if by a stylist, as Nieddu explains:

' [The Lyons] are famous. Jamal does have a stylist. He's a singer. He can't go shopping. He'll

be mobbed. Hakeem cannot go shopping. Like Kanye isn't going to the stores all the time. They can't. They don't have time.'

Although uniquely talented, when Jamal tells his father that he is going to come out, Lucious cuts him off without a penny, a plot line that challenges hip-hop's deeply rooted homophobia. In a flashback, Lucious thrusts a young Jamal in a bin when he sees him in his mother's heels. Cookie takes over as Jamal's producer and manager, eventually leaving Empire Entertainment to start her own record label, Lyon Dynasty. After allowing Empire Entertainment to acquire Lyon Dynasty, she returns to Empire as co-CEO and head of artists and repertoire.

The musical's soundtrack was executive produced by Timbaland. Various guest stars appeared as themselves including Gladys Knight, Mary J. Blige, Snoop Dogg, Rita Ora and Patti LaBelle.

I MAY DESTROY YOU

LYNSEY MOORE (2020)

A coruscating account of one woman's experience of rape and its aftermath, *I May Destroy You*, created, written and starred in by Michaela Coel, becomes a polemic against the sexual relativism inherent in contemporary sexual encounters and relationships. Throughout the series, East Londoner Arabella Essiedu (Michaela Coel), publicly celebrated Twitter star and author of *Chronicles of a Fed Up Millennial*, wears clothes that emphasise her need to prove her strength and physical presence: heavy-buckled boots, oversize textured and jacquard knits in bright colours, made more powerful by the insertion of shoulder pads, baggy high-waisted jeans or chinos pulled in at waist, tank tops and combat jackets resonant of 1990s girl band Eternal. Sourced in local charity shops and vintage stores, such as London's Portobello Road Market, Beyond Retro and Rokit, by costume designer Lynsey Moore assisted by Rosie Lack, the costumes reflect the daily garb of an urban millennial – denim jackets, graphic T-shirts and logoed athleisure – along with partywear of body-con dresses and sequinned bodices. Moore describes the creative process behind the drama:

> 'I love designing contemporary costumes because of the opportunity to present something new and share a new way of working. Unlike period design, there are no set rules in contemporary work. Just a massive amount of styles and characters to dream up.'

top left In a flashback to four months before the rape, Arabella and her friend Terry visit the Italian coastal resort of Ostia. Directed to the local baseball ground in pursuit of drugs, Arabella hooks up with Biagio (Marouane Zotti), a local drug dealer. Terry wears a jumpsuit patterned in an indigenous Dutch wax print from West Africa and faux-suede jacket. Arabella is off Insta-duty in a raw-edged, military-style khaki jacket partnered with strapped and buckled black shorts.

below left As Arabella goes through the recovery process, her look becomes less confrontational as she makes a concentrated attempt to capture an audience as an influencer. When the trio of friends embark on a shopping trip for Terry's birthday party, she wears a tracksuit by the mid-market athleisure brand Champion with a logoed cropped top and a new wig of hair that falls smoothly from a centre parting. Kwame (Paapa Essiedu) replaces his signature beanie for a bucket hat and wears a colour-blocked T-shirt. Terry French-tucks a print blouse into high-waist jeans.

opposite Exploring the devil/angel conundrum, Arabella chooses the dark-angel option – an angel combined with a dark demon, representing the dichotomy in her behaviour. Faux barbed wire is twisted around horns and around the waistline of a sheer black minidress from online retailer ASOS, which is worn over a black leather basque. Irritating her friends with her selfie obsession, she runs into the street, feverishly checking her Facebook Live for comments and reactions to her outspoken vilification of men.

Arabella is struggling to meet the deadline on her second book and is persuaded to embark on a night out with friends, culminating in her being drugged and raped. At first, her memories are hazy but, as she reluctantly comes to realise, the horror of the encounter, she begins to examine the nuances and limits of the various ways in which these boundaries are easily eroded through lack of self-esteem, passivity or insecurity. These can vary, and in one episode, a fellow writer Zain Sareen (Karan Gill), removes his condom while having sex with Arabella (in the United Kingdom, non-consensual condom removal is rape). When Arabella is invited to speak at a writers' summit, she names and shames him. The costume designer's intention in the scene is to offset Arabella's formidable military-style trousers and heavy boots with a fluffy mohair cardigan in a bid to confound the audience's expectations.

The series closes with several alternative endings imagined by Arabella: one of retribution for the rapist in which he is violently beaten to death and another in which she feels pity and takes him to her bed. She accepts the painful truth, however, that there can be no closure. Only by learning to accommodate the horror can she let it go.

SUCCESSION

MICHELLE MATLAND (2018–)

above A woman in a trouser suit subverts the norm of the alpha male. In 1848, there was a state-wide law in the United States prohibiting the wearing of dress of the opposite sex and it was still used in the twentieth century. However, the same language of power is at play whether male or female, as evidenced by Shiv and her brother Kendall. When the suit is cut to define the female form, both masculine and feminine attributes are present, thus combining Shiv's desire for power with an inherent femininity that she exploits in interactions with her father.

opposite The manner in which each character is presented is an indicator of their status in relation to patriarch Logan as they compete for his approval. Logan's body language is as intimidating as his pinstripe suit. In keeping with her Scottish heritage – and showing loyalty to her father, who was born in Dundee – Shiv wears a double-breasted coat dress in a muted Prince of Wales check, a woven twill that was originally known as Glenurquhart check.

Created by British writer Jesse Armstrong, *Succession* is a savage depiction of the upper echelons of power in the media industry. Set in a milieu of unassailable privilege, the saga traces the dynastic rivalries between the offspring of Logan Roy (Brian Cox), despotic patriarch of the Waystar Royco media empire. The youngest child is Siobhan 'Shiv' (Sarah Snook). In the first season, she alone among her siblings works outside the sphere of the family concern, as campaign manager for a rising liberal politician. Comfortable in her outsize knitwear and baggy trousers, by season two she is absorbed into the family enterprise where she develops a new, sharp corporate look and persona. Her weighty angled bob echoes the structured tailored pieces, in neutral that she wields alongside stealth-wealth knitwear.

As the ageing patriarch's health declines, Shiv joins the hierarchical fray with her brothers: Kendall (Jeremy Strong), the ex-addict heir apparent; Roman (Kieran Culkin), the youngest with a gift for toxic repartee; and half-brother Connor (Alan Ruck), the delusional dreamer on his private income. Shiv's freshly conceived ambition to run Waystar Royco is signified by her new wardrobe, sourced by costume designer Michelle Matland. For inspiration, the designer spent time observing the denizens of media-sector work-places in the United States:

'We would literally sit in their lunchroom [Viacom, Hearst, Fox], watch them come up in the cars in the

morning. The younger guys emulating the bigwigs.
But if you get up close you can see the bigwigs'
texture and fabric and cut are more expensive.'

As Shiv abandons the comfortable sweaters of her
independent era, she migrates to high-end labels such as
Stella McCartney, Gabriela Hearst, The Row and Armani.
Now a high-net-worth media executive, she reinvents
power dressing with a muted palette of greys, navy and
black, saving neutrals, cream and camel for her lighter
moments. Eschewing logos, printed patterns or bright
colour, fabrics are cut to drape; sweaters and trousers are
produced in the noblest of fibres from Italian label Loro
Piana, which specialises in rare raw materials such as
vicuna and first-grade cashmere.

Guided by wealth consultants, the production
unfolds in environments reserved for the uber-rich. This
drama of inheritance resonates with myriad, but elusive,
historic, contemporary and theatrical allusions, from the
Hearsts and the Murdochs to William Shakespeare's
King Lear (1606).

below Initially the favourite for the succession, a
drug-fuelled Kendall (left) compromises his chances of
advancement by causing a car accident in which a young
man is killed. He subsequently abandons his corporate
wear for more eccentric fashion choices, including the
Gucci bomber jacket he wears to his fortieth birthday
party. In a Monse asymmetric wrap dress in emerald-
green satin, Shiv abandons her delicate jewellery for a
statement gold necklace. Roman refuses to cooperate
sartorially in the celebration, remaining understated in
a blazer over a V-neck T-shirt.

Shiv is alternately favoured and dismissed, a victim of her father's capricious machinations. She is aided in her bid for power by her husband, the deeply unpleasant, sycophantic Tom Wambsgans (Matthew Macfadyen), labelled by *Atlantic* magazine as 'a smirking block of domestic feta'. Frequently humiliated by her, both socially and sexually, he in turn bullies his office subordinate, her cousin Greg Hirsch (Nicholas Braun).

Sharp tailoring, though widely *de rigueur* for the brothers, is not required by Logan to reinforce his authority. He favours a chunky, cable-knit cardigan with a cosy shawl collar when he is at his most malevolent. Only for the boardroom is he garbed in a bespoke suit, lined with Hermès scarves, by New York tailor Leonard Logsdail.

above left Following accusations of a cover-up of murder and rape charges committed on the Waystar cruise liners (an offshoot of their corporate empire), the Roy family get together on their mega-yacht to discuss damage limitations. The scene also provides an opportunity for Shiv to exhibit her summer wardrobe: a wide-brimmed sunhat from Brooklyn brand Lola Hats, the trousers from a pinstripe suit by the Ralph Lauren Purple Label worn with a sleeveless knitted top and Ray-Ban sunglasses. Although keen to present himself as laid-back and cool in his habitually too-tight shirts and chinos, Roman is nevertheless as ambitious as his siblings.

above right As her aspirations to become corporate head of the Waystar Royco empire begin to unravel, Shiv's high-style fashion sense becomes increasingly off-kilter. Under the blazing Tuscan sun, at the wedding of her cool and distant aristocratic mother, she begins to look uncomfortable in her clothes and wears an ill-fitting sheath dress with a pastel placement print.

above Within a favoured colour palette of pinks and reds, full-blown graphic tea roses form a leitmotif that runs through Madeline's wardrobe. A Dolce & Gabbana pencil skirt is harmoniously matched to a pale pink blouse with a frilled jabot, Prada handbag and patterned scarf. Compensating for her small stature, she favours cropped cardigans and figure-hugging, three-quarter-length coats.

opposite Immaculately suited, the high-powered CEO, Renata, is persistently volatile and on the edge of explosion. She predominantly wears structured tailoring, accessorised with stiletto-heeled shoes, to emphasise her rangey, gym-honed body. Popularised in the 1950s, the stiletto heel represents both femininity and power. Its invention is credited to Italian shoe designer Salvatore Ferragamo. The raw-edged, wool bouclé suit combines a judicious, below-the-knee pencil skirt with a collarless, drape-front jacket in a style reminiscent of Coco Chanel's classic cardigan suit.

BIG LITTLE LIES

ALIX FRIEDBERG (2017–2019)

Day one of first grade at the Otter Bay Elementary School provides the starting point for David E. Kelley's drama, *Big Little Lies*, adapted from Australian author Liane Moriarty's best-selling novel of 2014. The action is set against a West Coast backdrop of spectacular clifftop homes replete with glazed expanses of curtain walls, vast kitchen islands and infinity pools, and the characters have wardrobes to match. Even for the mundane task of the school run, they unhesitatingly draw on a uniform of high-end designer labels from the depths of their walk-in closets. The drama features the Monterey Five – Madeline Martha Mackenzie (Reese Witherspoon), Celeste Wright (Nicole Kidman), Jane Chapman (Shailene Woodley), Bonnie Carlson (Zoë Kravitz) and Renata Klein (Laura Dern) – as they deal with contemporary issues surrounding motherhood and marriage.

Costume designer Alix Friedberg won an Emmy for Outstanding Contemporary Costumes, in 2017, for her work on the series. She says of the show:

'Some characters aren't coping well with what happened and others are rising above it. We tried to reflect their emotional journeys through their costumes.'

The narrative is interrupted with asides, speculation and gossip from a group of witnesses to a murder; the victim is unknown until the final episode. Madeline is the acerbic

above With a theme of Audrey Hepburn and Elvis Presley, the school fundraiser and fancy-dress party sees a plethora of high chignons, little black dresses and Elvis lookalikes. Celeste's husband, Perry, is a threatening figure in black leather, while she pays homage to the film star and fashion icon in a tiara, a choker of pearls and a variation of the little black cocktail dress. First introduced by Chanel in 1926, it was popularised by Hepburn in an exquisite Hubert de Givenchy version in the romantic comedy *Breakfast at Tiffany's* (1961).

driver of the plot. She projects a resolutely feminine image, favouring fitted dresses in bold, floral prints, rose-strewn sweaters and spike heels. Whereas her first husband's younger second wife, the boho yoga queen Bonnie, is generally found draped in sustainable ethnic layers, with braided hair and turquoise jewellery.

The beautiful and vulnerable Celeste is ostensibly enjoying the perfect marriage to banker Perry (Alexander Skarsgård) and is a stay-at-home mother to twin boys. She wears soft, luxurious fabrics from upmarket labels such as Max Mara and Ralph Lauren. At home, her lissom body is adorned in a succession of silk and cashmere leisurewear and exquisite lingerie.

Renata provides the series with the familiar trope of conflict between high-powered, career-obsessed mothers and those that choose not to work outside the home. She represents her contempt for the latter with her predilection for hard-edged, high-luxe business attire.

By contrast, Jane is the dressed-down, combat-booted interloper who is a catalyst for change within the group. A single mother, she has moved from Santa Cruz to start a new life, only to have her son Ziggy (Iain Armitage) accused

at the end of the first day in school of trying to strangle Amabella (Ivy George), Renata's daughter.

Throughout the drama, as Ziggy begins to question his parenthood, Jane is beset by flashbacks of the rape in which her son was conceived. Celeste's husband proves physically and sexually abusive; it is only when she realises that one of her twins was responsible for bullying Amabella and copying his father's behaviour that she decides to leave him. Enraged by her decision, Perry begins a physical assault on Celeste at the school fundraiser and at that very moment that Jane recognises Celeste's husband as her rapist. Renata, Madeline and Jane attempt to intercede in his attack and, in the ensuing mêlée Bonnie, who has earlier seen Perry manhandling Celeste, runs and pushes Perry down a flight of stairs to his death. The women tell the police that Perry fell accidentally. They then attempt to get on with their lives in the aftermath of the murder.

above After the school drop-off, Madeline invites newcomer Jane to the local coffee shop to meet her friend, Celeste, and to rest her own sprained ankle. The status of the women is clearly defined by their clothes. Jane is relatively plain and low key, while Madeline exhibits her normal, prissily ornamented self. Typifying her role as former lawyer and the wife of a rich banker, Celeste wears an impeccable tonal palette of natural materials, from a camel wraparound coat, harmonising with her auburn hair, to her dark-tan knee boots in suede and a chestnut cashmere sweater with its long sleeves and turtleneck worn to conceal her bruises.

opposite above Madeline introduces Jane (right) to Renata at the school gates. Less affluent than the other women, Jane adopts a more casual, practical style of dress. She totes a hands-free, cross-body bag rather than a designer top-handle and wears a shabby, formless jacket and an unkempt pony tail. This contrast to the salon-maintained tresses of her general circle of friends leads Renata to assume that she is Ziggy's nanny, not his mother.

INDEX

PICTURE CREDITS

a = above; **b** = below; c = centre; **l** = left; **r** = right

Front cover
Omari Douglas as Roscoe Babatunde, still from *It's A Sin* (2021)
© Red Production Company & All3Media International

Back cover
Top: Liam Daniel/© Netflix/Courtesy Everett Collection Inc/Alamy Stock Photo **Below:** © BBC America/Courtesy Everett Collection Inc/ Alamy Stock Photo

Page 2 WENN Rights Ltd/Alamy Stock Photo **7** Sid Gentle Films/ Album/Alamy Stock Photo **9** Ali Goldstein/© Netflix / Courtesy Everett Collection/Alamy Stock Photo **10–13** Photo © Christophe Brachet **14** CBS/Not A Real Company Productions/Album/Alamy Stock Photo **15, 16a** Comedy Central/The Hollywood Archive/Alamy Stock Photo **16c** CBS/Not A Real Company Productions/Album/ Alamy Stock Photo **16b** Comedy Central/The Hollywood Archive/ Alamy Stock Photo **17** CBS/Not A Real Company Productions **18** Ali Goldstein/© Netflix/Courtesy Everett Collection/Alamy Stock Photo **19** Melissa Moseley/© Netflix/Courtesy Everett Collection/ Alamy Stock Photo **20a** Ali Goldstein/© Netflix/Courtesy Everett Collection/Alamy Stock Photo **20c** Saeed Adyani/Netflix/Kobal/ Shutterstock **20b** © Netflix/Courtesy Everett Collection/Alamy Stock Photo **21** Ali Goldstein/© Netflix/Courtesy Everett Collection/ Alamy Stock Photo **22** Two Brothers Pictures/Album/Alamy Stock Photo **23** Prod.DB © BBC - Amazon Studios - Two Brothers Pictures/ Alamy Stock Photo **24a, 24b** © Amazon/Courtesy Everett Collection/ Alamy Stock Photo **25** Two Brothers Pictures/Album/Alamy Stock Photo **26** © Netflix/Courtesy Everett Collection Inc/Alamy Stock Photo **27** Jax Media/Album/Alamy Stock Photo **28–29** Carole Bethuel/Netflix/Kobal/Shutterstock **30** © Netflix/Courtesy Everett Collection Inc/Alamy Stock Photo **31l** Abaca Press/Alamy Stock Photo **31r** © Netflix/Entertainment Pictures Alamy Stock Photo **32** Erik Pendzich/Alamy Stock Photo **33, 34l** HBO/Album/Alamy Stock Photo **34r** RW/MediaPunch Inc/Alamy Stock Photo **35l** Photo Gotham/GC Images/Getty Images **35r** Kristin Callahan/Everett Collection/Alamy Live News **36** Sarah Shatz/© Amazon/Courtesy Everett Collection/Alamy Stock Photo **37** Sarah Shatz/Amazon **38–39** Sarah Shatz/© Amazon/Courtesy Everett Collection Inc/ Alamy Stock Photo **40** Instar Images LLC/Alamy Stock Photo

41a 20th Century Fox TV/Album/Alamy Stock Photo **41b** Craig Blankenhorn/© Hulu/Courtesy Everett Collection Inc/Alamy Stock Photo **43** Andrew Eccles/Cw Network/Kobal/Shutterstock **44** Independent Photo Agency Srl/Alamy Stock Photo **45** Eduardo Castaldo/HBO **46, 47a** Landmark Media/Alamy Stock Photo **47c, 47b** Eduardo Castaldo/HBO **48** PictureLux/The Hollywood Archive/Alamy Stock Photo **49a** Everett Collection Inc/Alamy Stock Photo **49b, 50–51** © Netflix/Courtesy Everett Collection Inc/ Alamy Stock Photo **52, 53** Lifestyle pictures/Alamy Stock Photo **54** Landmark Media/Alamy Stock Photo **55** Eddy Chen/HBO Max/ PictureLux /The Hollywood Archive/Alamy Stock Photo **56–57** Landmark Media/Alamy Stock Photo **58** © WB/Courtesy Everett Collection Inc/Alamy Stock Photo **59** Everett Collection Inc/ Alamy Stock Photo **60a** Fox/Warner Bros. **60b** © WB/Courtesy Everett Collection Inc/Alamy Stock Photo **61** Fox/Album/Alamy Stock Photo **62** WENN Rights Ltd/Alamy Stock Photo **63** Storms Media Group/Alamy Stock Photo **64** Warner Bros. **65l** Everett Collection Inc/Alamy Stock Photo **65c** Giovanni Rufino/Everett Collection Inc/Alamy Stock Photo **65r** Landmark Media/Alamy Stock Photo **66–69** © EP Normal People Limited/Enda Bowe, 2020 **70** Lara Solanki/© Netflix/Courtesy Everett Collection Inc/Alamy Stock Photo **71** Adam Rose/© Netflix/Courtesy Everett Collection Inc/Alamy Stock Photo **72** Lara Solanki/© Netflix/Courtesy Everett Collection Inc/Alamy Stock Photo **73a** Ashley Beireis Nguyen/Photo 12/Alamy Stock Photo **73c** Tyler Golden/© Netflix/Courtesy Everett Collection Inc/Alamy Stock Photo **73b** Lara Solanki/© Netflix/ Courtesy Everett Collection Inc/Alamy Stock Photo **74, 75** Netflix/ Album/Alamy Stock Photo **76a** Jon Hall/Netflix/Kobal/Shutterstock **76c** Sam Taylor/© Netflix/Courtesy Everett Collection Inc/Alamy Stock Photo **76b** © Netflix/Courtesy Everett Collection Inc/Alamy Stock Photo **77** Netflix/Album/Alamy Stock Photo **79** BBC America **80** © BBC - Tiger Aspect Productions - Caryn Mandabach Productions. TCD/Prod.DB/Alamy Stock Photo **81** BBC/Album/Alamy Stock Photo **82a** Prod.DB © BBC - Tiger Aspect Productions - Caryn Mandabach Productions. TCD/Prod.DB/Alamy Stock Photo **82c** BBC/Album/ Alamy Stock Photo **82b** Prod.DB © BBC - Tiger Aspect Productions - Caryn Mandabach Productions. TCD/Prod.DB/Alamy Stock Photo **83** BBC/Album/Alamy Stock Photo **84–87** © X Filme Creative Pool Entertainment GmbH Degeto Film GmbH Beta Film GmbH Sky Deutschland GmbH 2017 - Fotograf Frédéric Batier **88a, 88b** © Frédéric Batier, X Filme Creative Pool GmbH, ARD Degeto

ACKNOWLEDGEMENTS

Writing this book has provided a fascinating insight into how essential fashion is in driving forward both character and plot in dramas on the small screen.

I would like to thank Kara Hattersley-Smith and my editor Carol King, whose suggestions greatly improved the book. Thanks are also due to Maria Ranauro for her tenacious picture research and Geoff Fennell for his wonderful design work.

Thanks too, to John Angus for his encouragement. The book is dedicated to my darling daughter Emily for her unwavering support.